This book is dedicated to the
three individuals who make my
life rich in the truest sense: My
wife Renee and my two
children, Ben and Jessica.

Published by 1 to Ponder
www.1toponder.com

Library of Congress Cataloging-in-Publication Data

Sher, Robert 1961-
        The feel of the deal: how I built a company through
acquisitions / by Robert Sher.
        ISBN-13: 978-1-60222-000-3
        ISBN-10: 1-60222-000-X
Library of Congress Control Number: 2007921899

Printed in Korea
by Hanjin P&C   www.hanjinpnc.co.kr

THE
Feel
OF THE
DEAL

How I Built a Company
through
Acquisitions

Robert Sher

Published by 1 to Ponder
2007

Contents

Acknowledgments.. vi

Preface... ix

Foreword x

Introduction.. xii

Chapter 1: Surviving Hello 1

Chapter 2: Conversation in the Cafeteria........... 8

Chapter 3: Dinner, Ginsburg Style 19

Chapter 4: A Surprise from Amsterdam........... 34

Chapter 5: The Blind Art Publisher 45

Chapter 6: The Dinner I'd Been Waiting For... 48

Chapter 7: Just the Facts, Ma'am.................... 65

Chapter 8: Painting the Picture of the Future ... 73

Chapter 9: Our First Offer 83

Chapter 10: Seller in Town............................... 94

Chapter 11: Strike While It's Hot.................... 123

Chapter 12: Attempted Murder....................... 134

Chapter 13: The Moment of Truth.................. 141

Chapter 14: Details and Deep Analysis.......... 148

Chapter 15: Essays on Business...................... 193

    Five Reasons to Extend Your Hand 193

Give First, Then Ask 197

The Benefits of Leading in Industry
Organizations...199

Get Out! 203

Inherently Wasteful 206

Tending to the Important 209

Good Reasons vs. Bad Reasons...................212

Outside Board of Directors..........................218

The Benefits of Peer Groups 225

How Deep in the Doghouse Do You Go? 230

All about Earn-Outs....................................235

Use of Advisors in Acquisitions...................239

Dealing with Banks 244

The Roving CEO 248

Staying Sane when Things Go Wrong 251

Afterword.. 255

About the Author 256

Acknowledgments

As always, it takes a lot of people—a team—to get many
of the really important things in life accomplished. Since
this is my first book, it is an important step for me in
many ways. Having grappled with the proper order in
which to acknowledge everyone, and the risk of burying a
name deep within a paragraph, I'll resort to a tool my
clients know I use often—a bulleted list. This one I'll put
in alphabetical order, rather than by priority.

Phil Ginsburg	How lucky I am to have bought a business from such an interesting, intelligent, warm and loyal man. Our friendship continues long after our business together has passed. He even calls occasionally just to encourage me to have a drink of Dewar's!
Jim Horan	A new mentor who not only has shown me the tactics of building a consulting practice around a book, but has been an unfailing cheerleader for me. So much more than the One Page Business Plan guy!
Harriet Rinehart	She was the owner of the first business I acquired. That experience may well have controlled whether I ever tried to acquire another business. She is an incredibly sensible, fair individual, and our deal came together so seamlessly and quickly that there wasn't enough content for a book! We're still friends 10 years later and her attitude and care for those around her is truly behavior worth modeling.

Mr. Dick Rutherford	My high school journalism teacher and newspaper advisor. The 2 ½ years I spent as editor-in-chief of the Wolf Print under his guidance was the impetus for making writing a life skill, a passion, and a tangible competitive advantage.
Rebecca Salome	The perfect editor for me—referred by Jim Horan—who has held me to high standards, kept me from making any rookie book-writer mistakes, and has guided me in my effort to make The Feel of the Deal something I am proud of and that will be effective.
Ben Sher	This eleven-year-old son of mine has amazing emotional maturity combined with the fire, passion and idealism that comes with youth. He's already contributing to those around him, and that includes me—he's given me the space to write this book and is fiercely supportive of me and his whole family.
Jessica Sher	My nine-year-old daughter may appear relaxed and easygoing, but her quick mind absorbs everything around her—both informational and emotional. When I least expect it, she synthesizes it at a level beyond her years and delivers pointed insights. She encouraged me to focus on this book and in her own quiet way helped me bring the project home.

Renee Sher	More than anything in my life, my marriage to Renee in 1992 and her unfailing support of me through thick and thin has made me who I am today. She believes in me and encourages me, and our partnership is everything I could have hoped for in a marriage. And of course, she's gorgeous.
John Weld	My longest-running mentor, who ushered me into teaching in 1995, who was and is my acquisitions coach, and whose counsel has been pivotal in my growth as an executive and as a person.
Paul Witkay	My involvement in the Alliance of Chief Executives has transformed my attitude about myself and my capabilities, and Paul's continued faith in and trust of me as my role at the Alliance changes is and will be instrumental in my success.
My Team at Bentley Publishing Group	Running an industry-leading company is never done alone. I must acknowledge the fantastic team that did the real work of getting us there. While the subtitle and the focus of the book is "How I Built a Company through Acquisitions," the truth is the company grew because of the excellent people on my team. Thank you.

Preface

In life, certain seminal events stand as important markers along our chosen path. Over a span of more than 20 years in business, acquisitions have been a significant force in my development, both as a person and as a CEO. Through it, I gained a new level of self-confidence. Acquisitions require such a breadth of talents and skills; each one presents an entire new world of unique challenges. And, as I have ventured in more than a few times, it is finally soaking in that I'm earning a new merit badge each time. Of course, I know I have many badges still to get, but every one gained takes me closer to the next one.

I'm a wiser, richer man for having seen up close how four other business leaders live their lives. Naturally, because I'm in business, I know many business leaders like me. But buying a business means diving in deep with another brave business owner like yourself, and being a part of their changing life as well as your own. It means baring your soul as much as you dare and seeing into theirs as much as they will allow.

Being a CEO isn't just my job or my career. It's a pathway through life that I have found to be full of stimulation, variety, challenges and gratification. My family and I have lived through one fascinating chapter after another. This book is one of those chapters.

Foreword

Few events create as many conflicting emotions as the sale of a closely held private company. Sellers feel they should be reimbursed for all the blood, sweat and tears that went into the building of their company, and can they be very emotional and irrational. Buyers are interested only in the future value of the company.

In this book, Robert Sher has shared the entertaining story of his acquisition of a key competitive firm in the art publishing industry. It offers us a rare opportunity to get inside the head of a CEO. Where most books about acquisition strategies stick to an in-depth discussion of the financial and strategic factors, Robert opens up his thoughts and feelings during the four-year journey that culminated in the acquisition. It makes for a good story, and a new kind of how-to guide—fun to read, and easy to follow.

The company that Robert acquires is not just a collection of products, customers and employees, but the life's work of a very passionate and talented individual. We get to "know" the seller quite well and find ourselves hoping for the best outcome for him as well as Robert. It is very important to the seller that his company is "adopted" by new owners that will respect his wishes.

What we have here is a wonderful story of how the emotional elements of an acquisition are intertwined with hard business analysis to result in a "win-win" result for both buyer and seller. But we also have the rigorous financial analysis used to determine the value of the company Robert is going to buy. His mastery then is the integration of story and facts—to create the "negotiating dance" that must take place between buyer and seller. Any business owner will be better for reading it.

Paul Witkay, CEO and Founder

Alliance of Chief Executives, LLC

Introduction

Buying four businesses is one of the most formative and interesting turning points in my CEO career to date. An acquisition really puts all the CEO's skills to the test—both the soft ones involving people and the hard business skills as well.

Buying a business can be a fast track to growth, and I love growing businesses. The company I led would not have gotten where it is without acquisitions. Every CEO should understand the value of an acquisition strategy. But acquisitions are not easy and often they do not end well.

This book shares what I did and what I learned. Rather than just lay out a prescription, I've decided to tell the story of my third acquisition. The story is fun to read and presents the context and emotion of the deal—which is of massive importance.

In addition to letting you see how a deal *feels* to a CEO, I've added end-of-chapter notes spelling out why I did what I did. In the last section of the book, I've included fifteen essays delving further into my thinking on topics related to acquisitions.

The story you're about to read is REAL, not a fable or fiction. I've changed only the sale price and a few other numbers to protect confidentiality. The seller's name has **not** been changed. Immediately following the story are several chapters that contain details about how I analyzed the business, what data-mining tools I used, and how I used them, as well as my report to my board to convince them to authorize the purchase.

Enjoy the 40-month-long view into my life as a CEO.

Chapter 1: Surviving Hello

Trade Show, Atlanta, Georgia, September 1997

Month 1

I pushed myself in. With hand extended and smile purposefully displayed, I stepped into my competitor's trade show booth. I offered, "Hello, I'm Robert Sher with Bentley, and I just wanted to introduce myself and meet you." *(For more on why this opening line works, read **A Great Opening Line** at chapter's end.)*

I could have done this at any of the past 15 years' trade shows, but hadn't. The Aaron Ashley booth had always been small, but very consistent. I knew their top sales guy by sight, but had never had any real conversation.

The older but self-assured man in the booth was polite and painfully concise. He replied, "Nice to meet you, I'm Phil." And that was it. No small talk offered. No clear path with which to carry on the greeting. Phil left it in my lap. He had that, "Why the heck is this guy here? What is he up to? He'll have to get there on his own," kind of look. Maybe he was wondering why, after 45 trade shows and 15 years, I decided to be friendly today, in September 1997.

I was there because our sales had slumped. Growth had been slowing, and now, two consecutive down quarters. We worried that our niche was going out of style, and one way to solve the problem was to buy another company with a different product mix.

This trade show was for the wall décor industry. My business, like Phil's, was art publishing. Briefly, this means we find artists that paint marketable originals, then get a license from them to reproduce their art as posters or prints. Then we resell those posters to picture framers large and small. Those framers frame the posters and sell them to very large chain stores, furniture stores, or through small custom framers.

This show had 40 or 50 booths with publishers just like us, but also had suppliers of picture framing molding, framing equipment, matting suppliers and more. Most buyers at the show were picture framers, both large and small.

There's always an excuse to talk to customers, but trade shows are one of the few times when competitors are naturally in close quarters, hence my attempted conversation with Phil.

My role as the CEO had always been the inside guy, and our outside guy, the sales director and a partner in the business, didn't believe in "talking to the enemy," so we had no relationships with competitors. When we started our business, we were a bootstrapping new entrant to the industry, and no one knew us. I assumed they wouldn't give me the time of day. But we had grown and had a much larger presence. I was learning that the tables had turned. Now far too many people assumed that *we* wouldn't give *them* the time of day, and so they were afraid to approach us.

But it was my turn to talk. I took the easy out. "So, how is the show going?" "Not bad." Phil responded, then clamped his jaw shut, looking me in the eye. Lovely. This was going really well. So I turned on a bit of monologue and detailed how the ebb and flow of customers had been at our booth over the past few days.

Then I decided to disclose something useful. Yes, to a competitor. I saw a key (but reclusive) buyer out of the corner of my eye.

I said, "Can you believe the Penney's buyer is here today? Has he stopped at your booth yet?" With visible interest, Phil said he didn't know him. I helped, "See that guy with the mini-recorder about 50 feet down the aisle coming this way? That's him. He was asking for some traditional botanicals, which we don't offer, but I think you do. Good luck: he's sort of an odd one. I'll swing back by later." As I scuttled out of the booth, I saw Phil's associate, who had been listening to us, move their collection of traditional botanicals to the front of the display bin. They beckoned to the big buyer as he approached. *(If you're wondering why I'd help a competitor, read **All about ME Doesn't Work Well** at chapter's end.)*

Having retreated to my own booth, six times the size of Phil Ginsberg's, I was distracted for several hours by customers. Truly I was distracted, because there are few things as exhilarating as the dynamic of selling—listening carefully for interest, then pulling the interest towards my products while dodging the objections tossed at me. At about 4:30 the dreaded "end-of-the-day lull" set in where buyers were in short supply. As I asked myself, "What shall I do now?" the immediate answer came, "Go back to the Aaron Ashley booth."

It's so much easier when you have an excuse. I had made my own with the tip about the Penney's buyer. *(Excuses aren't always bad, even though your mother may have said so. For my thoughts on a great use of excuses, read* **Find Reasons to Reach Out and Touch Them** *at chapter's end.)*

With good cheer displayed on my face, I rounded the corner, waved, and asked Phil, "So, how did it go? Did he actually talk to you? Usually he just mutters in his tape recorder as he sneaks by." (This buyer had a reputation for avoiding conversation and only collecting his own mutterings in his tape recorder.) Phil smiled, which was a welcome sign. He said, "We did actually get a few words out of him, and he seemed to like some of our things. Thank you." I could see in his eyes a visible shift from competitive suspicion to cautious warmth.

The conversation for the next few minutes was much more balanced, with Phil participating this time. It was useless show banter, just grabbing any topic available to hear each other talk, so we could size each other up. *(Chit-chat isn't always a waste. Read* **Doing Your Time—Face to Face** *at chapter's end.)*

4

I was feeling good that we had established enough rapport, so that six months from now at the next show, the stage would be set for deepening the relationship. *(I advocate having lots of shallow friendships. Read **Get to Know Them All** at chapter's end.)*

I was getting ready to exit, and then it happened. Phil said, "We should grab a bite to eat sometime." I was shocked, but hid it well. Clearly in such a short time, I had not done anything to justify being invited to share a meal. We were just in the early rites of getting to know one another, hardly having reached the "acquaintance" stage. Did he have some other agenda? Could it be that he was just a really social guy? My mind raced, but the half a second I had to think of the response was nearly over. I replied, "I'd like that. Have a good evening." Inside I wanted that meal to be *that* evening, but it would have been way too fast an approach. And that evening would be dominated by packing up our booths. The show was over.

Rob's Reflections: Chapter 1

A Great Opening Line
I first heard this line, "I'd just like to meet you, and have you meet me" on a sales training tape some 20+ years ago. The notion is that most people find it very hard to reject a person directly. If you come up with a reason for your visit, it's much easier to reject your reason than to reject you as a human being. You'll find a full essay on this subject on page 193.

All about ME Doesn't Work Well
Too many people start the thinking about making a connection with another with, "What can I get out of it?" Truly we are all self-motivated, but the overtly selfish approach is worn out. Make guilt your friend, and take a two-stepped approach. **Give first, then ask.** In the story I did this to break the ice when I pointed out a key buyer to Phil. You'll find a full essay on this subject on page 197.

Find Reasons to Reach Out and Touch Them
If part of your plan is to get to know as many people in your industry as possible, then be on the lookout for "excuses" every day. Look for things you observe that might be useful to others. After a round of sales calls, think about what information you could pass along to someone in the industry. Then pick up the phone and use the excuse to introduce yourself, or to reconnect. One of the best excuses is being involved in industry organizations. You'll find

a full essay on the benefits of being in industry organizations on page 199.

Doing Your Time—Face to Face

This comment springs from the part of the story where I was chitchatting with Phil—just talking for the sake of getting to know each other. I continue to be surprised at how important this is. As I am writing this book, I am having a series of meals with several people, making little progress at each. What is really happening is that we are accumulating "face time" and getting to know one another better. My sense is that the other parties have plans that they are not yet ready to reveal to me, but it's coming closer each time. A part of me would rather just discuss the opportunities, risks and rewards to see if there is even a chance at an immediate "deal." But it's not their way of working. Perhaps they have a string of possible opportunities in mind, and if there's no fit now, there are many other possibilities down the road—if they feel comfortable with me. I continue to invest the time because my sense of each of them (and my independent knowledge of the circles in which they travel) is that they are solid people, not just talkers.

Get to Know Them All

Creating shallow friendships with many people including competitors sets the table for an acquisition and puts you at the front of the pack. People prefer to do business with those they know. Cold call approaches are usually more difficult, can be slower, and are less likely to succeed.

Chapter 2: Conversation in the Cafeteria

Month 6

Six months flew by, and I thought about Phil and Aaron Ashley only a few times. No wonder. Within weeks I was in the UK at our first-ever international show. It was a disaster. We ended up in the wrong section, our presentation was confusing to Europeans (we did it American style), and we took only one small order on a prepaid basis, but the money never arrived. Skunked! There was one interested party that was persistent, our only glimmer of hope. (This interested party turned into our European distributor, then into our national sales director as well as my brother-in-law. Quite a good show outcome, ultimately, but it's quite another story.)

The quarter ending December, 1997 was horrible, down 16% over the same quarter a year prior, down from all the year's previous quarters, and for the first time in years, we had a loss. I do suppose that if you're going to have a loss, doing it debt free, and with a quick ratio of over 2 is the best way to do it. Certainly more comfortable than if you had debt repayments looming.

But the notion of becoming a smaller company over time was unsettling. Staying healthy as the business shrinks is hard work. Laying off staff and slashing any and every possible expense was not my idea of fun and did not figure into my plans for the future. It just wasn't me. I love growth and achievement, not mere survival. *(See

8

What Aspect of Business Do YOU Love? *at chapter's end.)*

As is always true in a downturn (ours was now three quarters long), you're never quite sure why. Is it the economy? Is it the industry? Is it our product category? Is it us? If it's us, is it pricing, product selection or our sales team? The biggest question is, "Is it permanent, or will it just go away?" *(For my perspective on dealing with soft sales, see **Why Are Sales Soft?** at chapter's end.)*

The top line in the first couple of months of 1998 was looking better—about even with the year prior. But of course, after 3 down quarters, I wondered if the good news was just temporary.

The upcoming show in New York was welcome. Although the days of getting a huge pile of show orders were long gone for our industry, it was still refreshing to get out of the office and meet with customers. Seemingly at every show, hope and opportunity arose, and some of those opportunities turned into real business in the months following. *(For my thoughts on how important it is to enjoy meeting your customers, see **Is It Refreshing to You?** at chapter's end.)*

Trade Show at Pier 98, New York City, March 1998
I used to hate uncertainty. It left me uncomfortable and unsure of what to do next. But some uncertainties are mysteries, waiting to be revealed. So it was with Aaron Ashley. During setup my memory was jogged about Phil's comments about having a meal some time.

Finally, in the early afternoon of the first day I found Phil in his booth. After some show chatter, I reminded him of his comment six months prior in Atlanta, and we agreed to meet the following day and walk over to the cafeteria together to share some overpriced food. We set the time for 12:30. I thought carefully about my objectives for this "meeting." They were simple.

Get to know him. It would have been nice to have a more defined strategy, but the truth was that while I had initiated contact, I didn't have full control over this. It was exploratory. I decided to be curious. I'd been in the business for only 12 years. Aaron Ashley had been in the business for 70 years—fertile ground for curiosity. *(For my thoughts on curiosity as a strategic tool during conversations, see* **The Curiosity of a Child** *at chapter's end.)*

We had a great hour-long lunch. I knew I was doing well because I finished my monosodium-glutamate-saturated faux Chinese food way ahead of him. He was enjoying telling me about the founding of his company. "I know I look ancient, but I'm not THAT old," he joked, reassuring me that he was "not dead yet." I registered his self-perception of his age. We traded lots of information, none of which was useful for day-to-day competition, all of which was excellent for understanding the context of each of our businesses. We both blended humility with pride in our companies. I was delighted with the relationship progress as I drained my Diet Coke and prepared to wrap it up. Then he did it to me again!

He chose the fast forward button, and said, "It seems that companies are combining in our industry. That being bigger has its advantages." "YEEHAAAA" screamed in my brain. The conversation was heading in a welcome direction, but the joy was dampened by the large decision tree I confronted as I looked for my next words. Singing the praises of largeness was what I wanted to do, but I needed to avoid insulting smaller firms, which I perceived (but didn't know for sure) that Aaron Ashley was.

I said, "Being bigger is better if that means that it makes life easier for the customer. Bigger is not better if it means slow, impersonal and inflexible responses." I continued, "But we have started to hear from our bigger customers a desire to reduce their vendor count, and as technology moves more deeply into our industry, some complex systems are easier to afford if you are a larger firm." I rested and waited for his response. I had the solution for Phil at the tip of my tongue (*sell your business to me*), but given his penchant for surprise in our conversations, and given my sense that he was not a man to push, I stayed silent.

Finally, he replied, "I can't disagree with that. But what is to be done? My sense is that you're already a larger firm, but we're not." I said, "Our plan is to grow aggressively. It is true that we are one of the larger firms already and are very sophisticated from an operations and IT perspective. Our biggest challenge is from a product-diversity perspective. We're known for a certain look and style. We are bringing out other styles of product, with only moderate acceptance. Frankly, we're not sure if the product is as good as it should be, or if customers aren't

11

used to buying such product from us. But we're publishing heavily. What's your plan to deal with the larger-may-be-better issue?" As I was speaking, I was toying with the idea of also saying that we were looking at acquiring companies to achieve that goal, which was sort of true (really we had only just talked about it but not pursued the idea actively—unless you call walking into Phil's booth "active pursuit"). But I didn't want him to feel pushed to the conclusion that I wanted to buy his business. It should have been obvious to him already, but I didn't know that for a fact. *(Read a critically important comment about keeping guesswork separate from fact:* **It's Not a Fact Until It's Proven** *at chapter's end.)*

Phil replied, "I have a young man in my office who is pushing me to do some product quite different than what we've always done. I like some of it. By and large, we are on a steady course forward. But I can feel the resistance in the marketplace, and on occasion, it's hard to get the attention of some of the new up-and-coming customers."

Whenever I've found myself trading information with a competitor, reading between the lines is critical. So far, it sounded like he was having a tough time, about twice as tough as the words would indicate. I decided to press on and be bold.

"Do you know much about New York Graphics Society? They bought several firms over the past five years. Do you think their strategy is working?" There it was. I had pulled the subject of acquisitions into the conversation, but from a third-party perspective. I figured it was safe. It was.

I learned that Phil was friendly with the owner of that firm and that they kept in contact. Phil seemed to think that the strategy had worked fairly well, although he got only limited bits of information about it all. Then, thankfully, he brought the conversation home.

"I'm not ready to sell (my heart was sinking) my business *yet* (now rising again)," Phil said. "If my kids had any interest in the business, it would be theirs. But there is no hope for that. We are healthy and profitable, and I've had offers in the past few years, some of them quite nice, and a few suitors are persistent. But I'm not ready. It has got to feel right for me, and it hasn't to date."

What do you say to that? Always, in conversations such as these, the pressing question is what to say next. Every word counts, and there are a hundred paths one can take to get to the end of the conversation. Some of them lead your way, and some of them will blow up. Many times, the shortest way to your objective is laden with hidden traps. I was convinced that this was the case. I went with my instincts, and chose *empathy*. I put myself in his shoes. *(Conversational skill is everything. Read **Show'Em You Have Ears and Are Willing to Use Them** at chapter's end.)*

"Phil, you've been running your business nearly three times as long as I've been running mine," I said. "The thought of selling is a huge life decision, and I think

13

you're right to wait until you're certain. And since the business is healthy, you can afford to wait."

I could see him reflect on his situation. I don't think he was wondering what to say to me, or what I meant. He was thinking about his company and his life, and about the choices that lay before him. Only a second or two passed, and lunch ended.

"Give me a call before Atlanta (the next show in six months), and let's grab a bite to eat." We cleared our trays, and headed back to the show floor.

Rob's Reflections: Chapter 2

What Aspect of Business Do YOU Love?

I love building businesses. That's great for me, but the real value of this comment to you is that you MUST understand what you love to do, and then focus on it and become really good at it. For those things that you don't love, find a way to have someone else (who does love them) do them well. Certainly there are plenty of times when you will not be able to delegate it all, and you will have to discipline yourself to do work you don't love. Even with the best discipline, you won't do the greatest job, and you'll be stealing time away from the area where you really can "make the magic." Are you sure you can't find a way to delegate your weaknesses?

Why Are Sales Soft?

Figuring this out is truly hard and sometimes impossible. But sitting at your desk wondering about it is not an acceptable research methodology. Face-to-face meetings with lots of customers where you ask them for their opinion on the industry is a great start. If you're friendly with competitors, ask them! Many will lie, but some will be honest. Even better, look at the competitors that seem to be doing well and compare and contrast them with everything you do. Most of the time, it's those differences that will reveal clues about why you are falling behind them, if in fact that is the whole problem or the problem at all. A sales slump can result from a combination of factors.

Is It Refreshing To You?

I hope getting in front of customers feels good to you. If not, caution is indicated. While there are a number of quiet, more introverted CEOs, enjoying customer contact and sales is a big advantage. If it's just not fun for you, you'll need someone you trust very close to you who does love sales, who is able to report observations without distorting them, and whom you'll listen to carefully. You'll find a full essay on the benefits of getting out of the office on page 203.

The Curiosity of a Child

Having the curiosity of a child is an incredibly powerful tool. Children (and I have two of them) ask questions without a clear motive. They do it for the sake of learning—so they can better understand the world around them. We don't suspect ulterior motives for their questions. This is contrasted with interrogation—a string of focused questions designed to extract the truth. People hate this—or even the feeling of this, especially when the aim of the questioner is not revealed. Questions born of child-like curiosity get people talking about themselves, which everybody loves. They'll walk away from a conversation feeling good about you because they got to talk about themselves. Of course if they talked most of the time, they won't know much about you, but trust me, they'll still feel good about you. Some enlightened talkers will sense when they are talking a lot and will seek to

balance the conversation by asking you questions—
the path to a great conversation for both parties.

It's Not a Fact Until It's Proven
I didn't want to act on the assumption that Phil knew
I was looking to acquire competitors, because I
didn't KNOW that this was in his mind. It was truly
my assumption. It is critical to keep clear on what
you know to be a FACT, versus what is a
HYPOTHESIS (a smart, but unproven deduction),
versus an ASSUMPTION (a complete hunch/guess).
This is not only important in conversations and
negotiations, but in all facets of business. A lot of
money is lost because we treat an assumption as
though it were a hypothesis, or worse yet, a fact.
This is so important that I should write an article on
this concept alone!

**Show'Em You Have Ears and Are Willing to Use
Them**
Most people do not listen well and don't really hear
what the other person is saying. But not you! So
when you hear something deep and emotional, it's
often good to reflect that back to the speaker.
They'll feel closer to you since you've made it clear
that you've understood them. In fact, you *will* be
closer to them for having understood them.

One way of such paraphrasing is to state your
reasons for agreeing with their position if you were in
their place, which is what I did in this story. I said,
"The thought of selling is a huge life decision, and I
think you're right to wait until you're certain. And

since the business is healthy, you can afford to wait."

Sometimes it means that you will validate a feeling they have, which is also an objection to the course of action you are pursuing. Although it feels counterproductive, such validation is the first step to neutralizing the objection with other facts or perspectives.

Chapter 3: Dinner, Ginsburg Style

It was crystal clear from our conversation that Phil was not about to hand me his business. But I wasn't in a huge rush either. Having never done an acquisition, I wasn't even sure that an acquisition was the right thing for the company. Intellectually, I couldn't justify spending time and energy on a competitor (as opposed to a customer) who had not made a clear decision to sell, or have any idea of his timeline.

But I liked him. He was a puzzle and was interesting. Most importantly, my gut told me that I should follow this thread and stay in touch. Why so much wisdom seems to reside in the gut is beyond me. But it seems to be true, so I often require my brain to listen to my gut.

Month 8

Off to conquer the European market we went. A new show was starting in Amsterdam, and we, along with lots of American competitors, were showing there. Our new relationship with a UK distributor allowed us to decrease our costs. My sales manager and I worked the show alongside our UK distributor. Or so was the plan.

The show organizers did almost everything right. They were gracious hosts, showing us the sights of Amsterdam on organized tours. (There most certainly are sights in Amsterdam: Prostitution and marijuana are legal, and in general, there is much less human inhibition in this city.) Our booths and the mechanics of setup were all in order.

They just utterly failed in marketing the show, so it was nearly devoid of buyers. We sat there, peering down empty aisles. This would be our second European show that could occupy the "complete waste" column on our show evaluation chart (if we actually had one).

In serious need of a silver lining, I sat there thinking, "So what is the best use of this time?" My mind dragged up an odd call I'd gotten a month earlier from Bruce Lieberman, a good customer for many years and a large distributor for all my competitors too. Bruce is a really nice person. He's an intellectual, who thinks about and analyzes everything that passes between his ears. This makes conversations with him particularly enjoyable. Of course, an unavoidable but positive side effect of being friends, or being friendly, or perhaps most importantly being respected by someone like Bruce, is that he is very well networked with the competition.

Sometimes it is a daunting task to know dozens or hundreds of people in an industry, especially if you are new. Befriending the ones who already know everyone, or better yet who influence many of them, is a great strategy.

He had suggested that I get to know Harriet Rinehart, owner of a small competitor I had not known much about but whose key product lines I was well aware of. When I pressed Bruce, he would say only that he thought I would like her and that our values were similar.

I pulled out the show guide and discovered that her firm was exhibiting at the show. Snidely, I told my sales manager to track me down if the booth got overwhelmed with customers, and seeing absolutely no one in the hallways, I walked off and introduced myself to Harriet. She was nice and pleasant, and we whined together about the lack of buyers, yet at the same time admired the generous entertainment provided by the show organizers. It was a short visit, and I returned to my still-empty booth.

Thankfully offsetting those long, quiet contemplative moments tending an empty show booth, our sales were up nicely in the second quarter. Ultimately we would finish it with record high sales for any quarter, nearly 15% up from the year prior. So we'd have the money to pay for this waste of a show. Being able to pay for a waste didn't really make the waste any better—because all waste feels bad to me. But it wasn't as grim. Was it a waste? Surely. But was it avoidable waste? Maybe not. For businesses to grow and expand, new things must be tried. The process of trying new things is inherently wasteful. *(You'll find a full essay on this subject on page 206.)*

The third quarter quickly unfolded and sales set yet another record, as did profits. We were swamped keeping up. Before I knew it, August was slipping by.

Month 11

As I began to verify my travel details for the next show, my mind drifted back to my plan to meet up with Phil at every US trade show, twice a year. With only two weeks left until show time, I called.

To my dismay, all his evenings were already booked up, and he didn't offer any lunch opportunities or try to stretch his schedule to accommodate a meeting. That might have been a bad sign—that he wasn't interested in continuing the conversation—or it might have meant that he was just busy. I quietly lambasted myself for being late to make the call. Phil suggested that I call him a bit earlier to set something up for the New York show six months away.

It is really easy to get swept away by all the *urgent* things in our day-to-day work, and forget about diligently, relentlessly pursuing the *important* things. Then we resentfully wonder how others around us with less skill and knowledge (in our opinion) seem to jump forward with big leaps of success. *(Why is this? You'll find a full essay on this subject on page 209.)*

Loathe to make the same mistake twice, I calendared my call to Phil for January, 1999, two months ahead of time.

Month 16

A dinner date was set. I was enthusiastic. It sounded like it was a one-on-one dinner. Since New York City was his turf, I left the details to him.

I had even more reason to be pumped up. Four consecutive quarters of sales growth were under our belt and all of them profitable. We had no debt, and although our liquidity ratios were slipping a bit, they were still way above anyone's definition of solid.

Statistics Show A Nice Upturn

	3rd Qtr 1997	4th Qtr 1997	1st Qtr 1998	2nd Qtr 1998	3rd Qtr 1998	4th Qtr 1998
Sales*	-7%	-16%	+2%	+14%	+8%	+16%
Profits	Strong Gain	Moderate Loss	Medium Gain	Break-even	Very Strong Gain	Small Profit
Debt	Zero	Zero	Zero	Zero	Zero	Zero
Quick Ratio**	2.9	2.4	1.9	2.4	2.2	2.3

* This period compared to the same period last year.
** Higher is better. Anything over 1.0 is good.

Month 18

As noon approached on the first day of the show, I realized our dinner was that night. Just as I thought about finding the Aaron Ashley booth and asking for details, Phil rounded the corner of my booth, gazed in for a bit, saw me, and approached.

"Good afternoon," he said, and continued without hesitation. "Let's meet at my home at 7:30 pm," and he handed me a slip of paper with an Upper East Side address. "Bring an appetite!" He extended his hand with a smile. "Nice booth," he complimented. "And busy too—this is my third trip over trying to find an opening to talk with you. For your sake, I sure hope they are really writing business. See you tonight." And he moved off.

He was in control of that conversation, and all I was able to do was say, "yes" "great" and "ok." I was fine with that, and certainly being invited to his home for dinner was fantastic. No objections from me at all! I also knew that Phil intended to be in control of that conversation and that he had the confidence to assert control. This dinner would be run on Phil's plan, not mine.

I did bring an appetite. The show had been really hectic, and a few bites of a sandwich was all there was time for at lunch. As an early riser, I tend to eat dinner much earlier than 7:30. I always found it odd (and still do) how much later Easterners eat dinner. Not to mention the fact that starting so late meant I'd be late getting back to the hotel, and after answering e-mails and reviewing show orders that day, I'd be in for a short night of sleep.

I stepped out of the cab just before 7:30. It was my first time in an Upper East Side neighborhood, with the stately, well-appointed buildings lining the street. Each had its awning with the doorman standing ready to help. Manhattan is expensive everywhere, but the Upper East Side is where the well-to-do live. Gripping my suburban mindset firmly, I thought about living in an apartment in a city—cramped, but energized. Would I want that?

The doorman showed me up, and Phil greeted me warmly, like a friend. After the jacket was off, and the tie removed (he insisted), he, as expected, offered me something to drink. It started like it does everywhere.

"What would you like to drink?"

Now I wanted to stay alert, and I'd never been much of a drinker (as in alcohol) and I didn't know where he stood on drinking, so I asked for my usual. "I'd like a Diet Coke if you've got one."

He started right at me, seriously, but with an expression displaying neither anger nor lightheartedness, and said, "What would you like to *drink*?"

I was clear to me that I had answered incorrectly. But it wasn't obvious at all to me what the right answer was. Feeling all too much like an awkward 12-year-old boy, I struggled for the right reply. Worse yet, Phil could see that I was struggling and was patiently looking me right in the eyes, waiting for a drink order that he was willing to accept.

Maybe he didn't have Diet Coke. I broadened the request. "Oh, I'll take any soft drink you have in the house, or ice water is fine too."

Phil's head recoiled ever so slightly, still with no sign of anger, but more a sense of resoluteness to hear what he wanted to hear. He replied, "I said, what do you want to **drink**?" with even more emphasis on the word *drink*. Then I got it, finally. He wanted me to choose a drink with alcohol. Worried that I was too thickheaded to get his hint, he added, "We do serve alcohol here."

The sense of relief in getting help to uncover the meaning of the riddle was quickly offset by having to make the *right* choice of alcoholic beverage. Being pretty close to a non-drinker (at that time), my knowledge of drinks was quite slim. Embarrassingly slim. Being embarrassed slows the mind. When my brain finally kick-started, I

pretty much had to say the first thing that came to mind—
one of the first drinks I had imbibed as a teenager. "How
about a rum and Coke?" I offered. Oops. A look of
disgust, coupled with a look of paternal pity, crossed his
face.

So the gig was over. I hadn't measured up to this 70-
year-old on the "manly drinking front" and would now be
relegated to the "youngster-that-needs-to-be-trained"
category. Not that this was a bad role to take when
dealing with any person nearly double my age. *(For some
thoughts on the value of role playing, see **In What Role
Does This Act Cast You?** at the end of this chapter.)*

"How about a Scotch," Phil guided. I was thankful now
that he would point the way, so I wouldn't have to suffer
any more embarrassing guesswork. "Do you enjoy
Scotch?" I knew now that Scotch was the right drink, and
that I would be drinking it tonight. I scrambled for the
right answer again. "My Chairman enjoys Scotch, and
I'll bet I will too. What would you recommend?"

"What Scotch does he drink?" Phil inquired. "Cutty
Sark," I replied. "I would NEVER even have Cutty Sark
in my home," Phil assured me. "I will pour you a
Dewar's on the rocks, which is what I am drinking. After
that, I will switch you to Chivas Regal, my second
favorite, so you can compare the two. Please sit down."
And down I went into the large chair in the living room.
For a minute, I had the chance to think about what to do
next. I was rattled, and decided to just go with the flow.
The Dewar's certainly would help that along!

With drink in hand, he gave me a tour of his home. Not an apartment at all, but a 2500+-square-foot duplex, nicely appointed. Phil introduced me to his two beloved Bichon Frise dogs and with great pride showed me how disciplined the fluffy white animals were to eat from only *one* of his hands.

He showed me his workshop where he cut figures from plywood with a scroll saw in the evenings, and told me that I would be choosing one of the dozens on the shelf to take home. I chose an eagle and keep it displayed in my office.

He showed me pictures of his grandson, whom he had dubbed, "The Prince," and he showed me his photography hobby, mostly focused on his family. And then there was the dollhouse he was making for Gracie, his other grandchild. *(It is useful to note what is meaningful in life to someone. If everything is about how much money they can earn or save, your negotiation with them will be more difficult.)*

I also saw the gallon-size jug of Dewar's from which my glass had been filled, and it became quite clear that drinking in this home was more than just occasional.

Of course, this didn't all happen without a refill of Dewar's. Phil was not showing a single sign of alcohol in his behavior. I was hoping that I too was acting sober, but I could feel the alcohol taking effect. As a nearly non-drinker, I had no physiological tolerance and was trying hard to slow down—especially when I realized that an empty—or even partly empty—glass was not going to be tolerated.

Phil's wife Rachel had responded orally to Phil's loud, bellowing call for her to come down and meet me, but she had not appeared yet. Finally, we made it back to the living room, where I sat down, grateful that I could not stagger while sitting. Phil left to get some appetizers and returned with them along with instructions about defending the appetizers from the two Bichons, who looked longingly at them.

I looked longingly at the food too—not only was I hungry, but I knew enough about drinking to know that food would help offset the effects of the alcohol, which were quickly growing. Trying not to look like a starving animal, I worked away at the nuts and cheese and crackers. Phil didn't touch them at all, even as he drained his third drink. He didn't look the least bit intoxicated.

I learned that we would be accompanied by Phil's Spanish distributor—a firm I'd heard about but had never done any business with. I thought it a sign of trust that he would mix me, a competitor, with a customer. At 8:15 the Spaniard arrived with his aide, who spoke English more fluently. Another round of drinks flowed. The Spaniard had been a guest many times before, so his preferences of *drink* were already known. He wasn't put to the test as I had been.

Then Phil remembered—he hadn't played us Beethoven's Ninth Symphony, which he had really been enjoying recently. He jumped up and moved over to where his stereo system was hidden in a cabinet. "You've got to hear this," he said, as he cranked up the volume and pressed play. As the full-bodied sound of the orchestra permeated the room, he faced us and closed his eyes, sinking into the music. His hands started moving as though he was conducting the orchestra. The moment lasted only 20 seconds, then he awoke from his trance, turned the music off and commented, "Isn't that great!" He announced that it was time for dinner. We all rose.

Having neither smelled nor seen any cooking activity since my arrival, I had figured out that we were only meeting at his home. Well, that's not true. There were two activities that night at his home—as there would be on every night over the years when I would dine with Phil. The first was always greetings and conversation, and the second was drinking.

That Phil is a unique character goes without saying. He is passionate about many things and is uninhibited about sharing them. Whether it's his love of a good drink, his grandchildren, his music, or any of the other things I learned about him that night, he is not embarrassed to exhibit his joy for life. His business was just one of those things.

To conclude that Phil was a wild man, talking and showing off but not observing each person around him would be wrong. I suspect that people react quite differently when exposed to Phil's strong presence, and that Phil monitors those reactions carefully on his path to deciding how well he likes and trusts each person. I was clearly off balance, as the evening was proceeding in a fashion that was outside my experience to date.

So I did the only thing one can do when you're not sure what you *should* do. I was just going to be myself, but on the quiet side of normal. Just roll with it and see how it all turned out. There would be less chance of slurring my speech as well. *(What do you do when you are clueless about a conversation? Read **Should You Be Naive or Chicken?** at chapter's end.)*

After another yell from Phil for his wife Rachel, she descended down the main stairs. A lovely Southern woman, graceful and warm, she greeted us all. Phil hosted us at one of his favorite restaurants, and we conversed about a variety of light topics. He made a special effort to make the Spaniard comfortable and to include him in the conversation. It was interesting to see the obvious mutual friendship they felt for each other, despite what appeared to be a large language barrier.

Phil made another drink or two unavoidable at the restaurant, but the big juicy steak I ate (Phil strongly recommended one in particular, so I chose it) did its job of offsetting the strongest effects of those drinks.

At about 11, the dinner wound down. Having been worried that we would end up going back to his home for a round of after-dinner drinks, I was relieved to learn that we would all catch cabs outside the restaurant to head directly to our hotels. *(I had no way of knowing then, but Phil's drinking is carefully controlled by a self-imposed regimen. He never starts before 6 and never drinks late in the evening.)*

As he succeeded in flagging one down for me, he thanked me for coming and told me that he thoroughly enjoyed my company. As he gave me a double-handed shake, he said, "Let's do this again." I concurred.

Rob's Reflections: Chapter 3

In What Role Does This Act Cast You?

In every relationship we take on a role. Figuring out what that role will be for you to create the best relationship is important. I don't mean that you should be "fake" or try to be someone that you aren't. Think about how differently you relate with a spouse versus a parent, versus a child. It's still all the same you, but in different roles. In this case, playing the role of top dog was not going to work, and that particular role is not one I play often. I would be playing the role of student in many respects with Phil, as I had many things to learn from him, and he enjoyed teaching them. Being a student in some areas had no negative effect on his level of respect for me in my areas of strength.

Should You Be Naive or Chicken?

Admittedly, there is a part of me that is uncomfortable appearing naïve. I would rather have experience in everything, so that I know what to do and how to act. But that's impossible. The question, then, is how to act when you don't know how to act. One option is to pretend to know what to do, but the likelihood of being called on it is high, and then it becomes obvious that you were too "chicken" to admit lack of knowledge. The best posture is to be both curious and interested in what you don't know. You learn more, and it makes the other person feel wise, as they get to be helpful. It is possible that they could look down their nose at you for being so naive, and if they do, it portends a rocky relationship with little value anyway.

Chapter 4: A Surprise from Amsterdam

After the dinner with Phil, two more days of show followed. As always, I tried to get out of the booth to see my fellow exhibitor's displays. As I passed by the Rinehart Fine Art booth, I renewed my introduction with Harriet Rinehart and chatted for a few minutes again. The conversation was not memorable, but she seemed nice enough. Harriet didn't even enter my mind again until she called in early April, 1999.

Month 19

She reminded me that we had first met in Amsterdam. There was an odd, uncomfortable pause, and then she said, "Have you ever thought about buying another publisher's business?" *(Friends First, Cash Second will shed some light on my style of finding buyers. It's at chapter's end.)*

And the discussion began. She was ready. I was interested.

Month 21

By June of 1999, the deal was done. Bruce was right—we were quite compatible. I learned much through this first acquisition of mine, but it would be wrong to dive into the Rinehart story and hijack the story I have already begun to tell. As June closed, trucks were rolling westward with inventory and the press releases were sent off.

I could no longer call the Amsterdam show a complete loss! If I hadn't gone to that terrible show, this first and pivotal deal might never have happened. *(Trying New Things at chapter's end talks about the high costs of experimentation in business.)*

It was a pivotal deal for a number of reasons. It was our first and we had successfully done it—successfully negotiated the deal. We also successfully integrated the operations and we kept the customers happy. Many businesses fail in the integration stage. I wasn't worried about it because I enjoy operations as well as sales and strategy. It was hard for us, however, and took a lot of energy and focus.

It was pivotal also because we'd kept the seller happy. I had understood what she wanted to do going forward and found a way to make that happen. We were paying her on time, and she was fitting into her new role well. Word about all of this was out in the industry and was setting the stage for what was to come.

We were also learning a lot about a different product category and were seeing the sales dollars roll in on things that we wouldn't have thought to work in the marketplace as we had understood it. *(Those Who Sell Their Businesses Are Not Necessarily Inferior! Read this humbling lesson for sure—at chapter's end)*

It was clear that the Rinehart name had brand equity, and keeping that product line differentiated from our own product line would be beneficial. We became a two-brand company. *(Cherish the Brand Equity You Buy. Find out why at chapter's end.)*

Month 24

September, 1999 marked the Atlanta show again, and I looked forward to my encounter with Phil. His #1 man, Henry Kuver, had stopped by the booth and told me to meet Phil at his hotel room before dinner. I had learned that Phil for many years had the benefit of only one working eye, and that this one good eye had begun having problems. He would not be spending much time on the show floor. Illness, disability and death are some of the biggest reasons that businesses get sold. If I were a cold-hearted enough person, I would have been glad for this news. But Phil had become a friend, and the thought of his being sightless was quite sad. *(You'll find a full essay on the subject of good reasons versus bad reasons on page 212.)*

As I knocked on his door, I wondered what Phil would be like off his home turf. He invited me in warmly. The dinner and evening were much less theatrical and much more personal. We learned a lot about each other's family and background. I learned a lot more about the anatomy of the eye and his hopes and worries for his eyesight in the future.

I never did see him come down to the show floor. He called me in November to tell me that he had elected to undergo eye surgery on his good eye.

Month 27

The Rinehart deal propelled growth even more, and the end of the fourth quarter found us up 22% over the same quarter a year prior. That, combined with all the IT preparation for Y2K had kept everyone running. By mid-January, the sense of normalcy was just starting to return to the company. I was really enjoying being an acquirer and was wondering when Phil might be ready to sell.

In one of our regular conversations, Harriet asked, "Do you know Leslie Levy Publishing?" I knew of the firm and had been generally friendly to the petite owner of the Arizona-based niche publisher. Harriet went on, "She called me the other day to check up on how we were working together and how my sale went overall. It turns out that she is growing tired too and is interested in selling. Shall I put you two together?" *(I assure you you'll place A **Truly Good Partner Plays for the TEAM** in front of somebody that you know. At chapter's end.)*

Month 31

I don't have to tell you what the answer was. By April 2000 we had closed the books on our second acquisition. Leslie too stayed on in a role that she was interested in, and we kept all our promises. Keeping promises fit with our value set, but it also built our reputation as a good acquirer. *(**Happy Sellers Beget Eager Sellers** shares the truth about the power of reputation in M&A deals, at chapter's end.)*

With three brands in the family now, we created a corporate brand umbrella (Bentley Publishing Group) and began billing ourselves as three publishers in one. The generally complimentary chiding began, "You're buying up everybody," which was hardly the case, but it was a great, strong perception to have out in the market.

We also joined the world of being a borrower again, having been able to fund one acquisition from cash flow, but not two. The leverage was slight, but real. The liquidity ratios had fallen from incredible to normal. Operating margins had thinned but were still positive. The cost of absorbing both acquisitions in the same fiscal year was significant and noticeable on the financial statements. *(**Getting Comfortable with Debt?** Be warned at chapter's end.)*

Somewhat disturbing was that revenue growth from our core product line was gone, and the sum of the two acquisitions plus our own business was less than the total revenue added at the time of the deals. Whether this was caused by the acquisitions, or whether our core business would have shrunken anyway was a source of debate. *(**The Total vs. the Sum of the Parts** is a story few want to hear, but it's at chapter's end anyway.)*

Notice the Financial Trends

Nice sales growth, thin profitability, declining liquidity and borrowing begins.

	3rd Qtr 1997	4th Qtr 1997	1st Qtr 1998	2nd Qtr 1998	3rd Qtr 1998	4th Qtr 1998
Sales*	-7%	-16%	+2%	+14%	+8%	+16%
Profits	Strong Gain	Moderate Loss	Medium Gain	Break-even	Very Strong Gain	Small Profit
Debt	Zero	Zero	Zero	Zero	Zero	Zero
Quick Ratio**	2.9	2.4	1.9	2.4	2.2	2.3
Event	Met Phil					

	1st Qtr 1999	2nd Qtr 1999	3rd Qtr 1999	4th Qtr 1999	1st Qtr 2000	2nd Qtr 2000
Sales*	1%	+10%	+6%	+22%	+28%	+8%
Profits	Medium Gain	Medium Loss	Small Gain	Break even	Moderate Gain	Small Gain
Debt to Equity***	Zero	Zero	Zero	Zero	Zero	.57
Quick Ratio**	1.6	1.25	1.03	1.05	1.12	0.82
Event		Bought Rinehart				Bought Levy

* This period compared to the same period last year. Sales numbers include sales from acquisitions after the deal was consummated.
** Higher is better. Anything over 1.0 is good.
*** The higher the number, the more the debt.

Regardless, we had gained 8% in overall sales. We were experienced in integrating competitors, we had a reputation as an up-and-coming publisher, and we had two happy sellers. My staff was entreating me not to buy any more businesses—they were tired. I told them not to worry. But of course, I had no real control over opportunities that might be presented to me.

Rob's Reflections: Chapter 4

Friends First, Cash Second

I've never called up a business owner and offered to buy their business. But six times I was approached, and I bought four times. Much of this happened after we established a reputation for being a good buyer. I'm not against approaching businesses. Crafting a plan for a series of acquisitions is probably the best approach, because you will be acting strategically, rather than opportunistically. I still favor a soft approach, developing some level of a relationship before pounding on the door and offering loads of cash.

Trying New Things

Trying new things in business is costly. The short-term effects can be negative. You often don't get what you set off to achieve. This reality must be drilled into the heads of your board and your entire team. Their orders must be to try and achieve the objective, but at all times to have their minds open and their radar seeking ANYTHING that could bring value back to the organization. New activities for a business are scouting missions. Stay alert, and send creative and open minded people on the missions.

Those Who Sell Their Businesses Are Not Necessarily Inferior

This is huge. There are some things one can learn about a competitor from the outside if you pay close attention. But actually buying the company opens the door for growth. Too many people on the buying side assume that because the seller sold, they are "inferior" and that their ways are all inferior. This is not true at all.

There are hundreds of reasons why a business may be sold; only some of them relate to poor practices in operations or product selection. Even if some of what they do is less effective than the acquirer, many of the things they do will be better. Maybe it's how they pack their boxes, or how their warehouse is arranged.

It is critical to listen to how they do things and absorb as much of the accumulated knowledge they have developed over the years. After you have that knowledge, and only after, can you compare the value of their method to yours, and choose the best.

In the case of Rinehart, her eye for art was different from ours. We had indisputable proof that her eye was effective, because we saw the posters rolling out the doors every day. We had to re-educate ourselves to her kind of art, lest we start rejecting marketable images because they didn't conform to our old comfort zone. We even gave her, contractually, the right to override our art selection rejections (with limitations if her picks didn't sell) so as to insure that her taste could still get to market. Harriet and I called it the "Crazy Harriet Fund." We still laugh about it today.

Cherish the Brand Equity You Buy

It takes forever to get customers to change their impression of a company. For most small firms, your brand is your company. So when you buy a successful company, it's often best to maintain the brand image and harness the position it has in the buyer's mind. One option is to grow the brand, keeping it very separate from your brand. This means investing money in that brand in many ways. Other strategies keep the brand alive but not promoted heavily—allowing the brand's perception to slowly graft onto the acquiring firm.

A Truly Good Partner Plays for the TEAM

Harriet's referral of another acquisition candidate was not in her best short-term interest. It would decrease our focus on the product line bearing her name. It would increase the competition for our publishing budget, meaning that she would get a smaller number of products going in print that would pay her a percentage. Finally, it would decrease our dependency on her for artist recruitment. Why then would she do it? The answer is that our relationship was one of helping each other succeed. We were partners, in the non-legal sense, and good partners help each other even when it doesn't directly help them. Cumulatively such an attitude and behavior set creates intense mutual loyalty, which is often undervalued by those who don't understand how this works.

Happy Sellers Beget Eager Sellers

The notion of building a reputation as a good acquirer is a critical one. A good reputation really has two components. First is that you are in fact a "good" person and company. Second is that people *know* about the good you did. The second part is the easiest, since acquisitions are talked about a lot and are of great interest to most business owners. Even more, all the customers of the acquired firm see just how well the integration went, based on how they were treated. The most important opinion, however, is the seller's opinion.

Do the following:
- Pay them as agreed.
- Treat them with respect.
- Take good care of that which they care about (their business, perhaps some key employees).
- Hold up your end of the agreement.

Do this consistently, and word will spread. You can even ask them to spread the word. You can bring them to industry events, where everybody can see them with you, looking happy.

In a series of deals, there will always be some bumps which will leave some people feeling unhappy. Their stories will damage your reputation as an acquirer, so bear that in mind as you deal with their issues. However, the stronger your reputation as a good acquirer, the more easily they will dismiss the few "bad" stories as untruths and not being your fault.

Getting Comfortable with Debt?

Intellectually, I know that debt, or leverage, is a great way of increasing ROI, and that debt has a place in financing. I also know that debt is often a way of financing adventures that the business can't really afford. If those adventures pay off as planned there is no problem. It's when they don't that it gets sticky. Worse, if the entire company starts losing money, then the leverage can be deadly. Debt is a valid business tool, but don't ever get too comfortable with it.

The Total vs. the Sum of the Parts

Most of the time, when two businesses come together, their combined sales never equal the sum of the two separate businesses. That's a real drag, but it's true. Some of it is the friction of an acquisition. Some of it is the distraction of both firm's teams while they re-learn their jobs and manage the extra work of putting two businesses together. Some of it is a less-focused strategy. Some of it is a mystery. Just be sure when you forecast post-acquisition sales that you knock off some percentage points from the sum of the parts.

Chapter 5: The Blind Art Publisher

After the eye surgery, I kept in touch with Phil monthly. It wasn't going well, and while he really seemed to keep his positive attitude, his ability to function at work was bothering him. It was difficult to read and even harder to judge color. He began referring to himself as the first-ever blind art publisher. I did what I could to keep him cheery, but the doctors were in unknown territory with Phil's condition, and the prognosis never got any better than uncertain.

Month 35

Early in August, 2000 Phil called to set a date for dinner at the Atlanta show the following month. He wasn't hopeful about his eyes and commented that he wasn't sure he was able to put the energy and focus into Aaron Ashley that it required. He suggested that the time for him to sell the business might be coming closer, but he hadn't made any decisions about it yet.

My counsel was the same for Phil as it was for anyone. That selling a business he had run for so long was a huge decision and should be made only when Phil was really certain. If the business was healthy, then there was no reason to rush the decision.

Interestingly, Phil disagreed with me. He talked about how every business needs attention, and he wasn't feeling up to it.

Isn't it a crazy thing? The more I told him he didn't need to sell the business (to me or anyone) the more Phil wanted to move the sale forward. It was as though I was arguing on Phil's behalf, and he was arguing on mine. But this is one of the big truths about negotiations and trust. If the other party feels that you have their best interests at heart, they, in turn, will try to have your best interests at heart. But the minute they sense that you're all about you—all about your winning and their losing, then the trust vanishes and the negotiations grow hard.

I said, "Phil, it's up to you if you want to talk about this in Atlanta. I'm in no rush. But if you think you might want to, it is only prudent that I be bound by a confidentiality agreement. I've got the one I used for my past two acquisitions that is balanced—it requires that both of us keep matters confidential. I'm happy to send it to you, and if it looks good, we can execute it before we travel to Atlanta, so that we're free to talk about this when we have dinner."

After a pause, he replied, "Well, there's no harm in that. Please send it over."

And I did. We signed it, exchanged copies on August 17, 2000, but spoke not a word until the show. The month's silence left me wondering about what would happen at that dinner.

The opportunity to buy a company with steady sales and a long history of profitability was exciting. Of course, it wasn't happy news that Phil was anticipating a growing disability rather than an easygoing retirement. I was concerned for him as a friend yet delighted as an entrepreneur.

I had to control my excitement with the knowledge that he might very well decide to keep the business for another few years. I recalled all too vividly 20 years earlier when I had made my first acquisition approach. The target was an elderly founder, running a small business. The talks went on for quite a while, and then, at the eleventh hour, emotions took over and the seller unceremoniously pulled out.

There wasn't much time for musing. Two new acquisitions and the demands of a growing business kept my mind from ever being idle.

Chapter 6: The Dinner I'd Been Waiting For

Month 36

The number two man at Aaron Ashley was Henry. He'd started working there as a very young man, and 42 years later, he was still at Phil's side. I didn't know Henry well yet, but it was obvious he was a sincere, dedicated man. At this show, he had been sticking even closer to Phil to be sure Phil could get where he needed with such poor vision. He gave me the details I needed to get to the right room in the adjacent Omni hotel and reconfirmed the time with me. In the end, we walked up together. It was September 16, 2000.

In his hotel room we exchanged light banter, and I inquired about his eyesight problems. Overall, he seemed to be the same Phil as always and quite upbeat. He announced that he would treat me to Morton's (an upscale restaurant known for its meat), and we set off to walk there. Henry went off with another Aaron Ashley staffer.

We arrived, and Phil produced his Morton's membership card. It was my first time eating at Morton's, which is not for the budget conscious. Obviously, Phil ate there often, and it reminded me that Phil was not poor, not that he had ever claimed to be. It was interesting that I was in fact surprised he was in the Morton's club, since I had long ago learned that Phil never ate dinner at home—he ate out 364 days per year—with the exception of Thanksgiving, which was actually cooked in the New York duplex's kitchen.

I had no intention of bringing up the question of acquisition to Phil. Our conversation of a month ago, and the signing of the NDA (non-disclosure agreement) was enough to set the stage. Knowing Phil as I did, it was up to him to decide when the right moment arrived. I should have guessed that it would be related to drinking.

The drinks arrived, and Phil took control of the toast. He said, "To celebrate my decision that the time has come to sell Aaron Ashley to you. To our deal!"

What delightful words! I got very excited and he could tell. So much for being a poker player. But the excitement was good. It let him know that I regarded Aaron Ashley as something I wanted to be a part of, and something to respect. I suppose if Phil had been a hard, cold seller interested only in the money, my reaction might have raised the price. But we had a relationship, which gave Phil the comfort that I was the right buyer, that I was his preferred buyer, and that I was honest. Displaying some real emotion—in the form of excitement—was real and it was honest. Phil liked seeing my excitement.

I honestly don't remember exactly what I said after the toast. The emotional high that accompanied the news lasted for a few minutes at most, then my brain had to manage the task of dinner and the discussion.

Like most CEOs, I am action oriented. My heart wanted to take action now, to negotiate the deal, and take the company home, just like a watch, or a new computer.

It doesn't work that way. He who rushes the process loses. Buying and selling companies takes time, and the deal must evolve as the parties learn what they need to learn, and emotions and positions shift with time and pressure. I checked myself and began asking very general questions about the company—products, confirming key customers (we all dealt with many of the same key customers), employees, and so on. I also asked and received some of the key numbers like sales, profits, COGS and other key costs.

What does he really want? That was the question that kept pounding away in my head. And it was not just the money, although that was a huge part of it. But it was all the other things that, in most cases, actually get the deal done, and for an amount of money that makes sense. Although all the acquisition negotiations that I had decided to pursue had concluded on good terms, I'd heard stories about the incredibly high percentage of deals that fall through—especially when the emotions of a longstanding owner are involved.

That Phil was not desperate for money was a good thing for the negotiations in the one sense—he would want to get the deal done on reasonable terms. But he ran a good business, and this last sale would be no different from any other of his more regular business transactions—he would demand a fair price for the value he delivered.

As they wheeled over the cart of meat from which we would choose our actual steaks, we noticed that five tables over was the CEO of one of the larger firms. Hal was a big man, whom I had never met, so Phil launched into how much he'd enjoyed shaking the man's hand.

Phil was enthusiastic. "His hand is so big it's like a baseball glove!" I smiled, more worried about being seen dining with a competitor and the fact that gossip about it might travel through the industry, or if we could somehow be overheard. Having acquired two firms already, I knew some talk was already circulating. But there was nothing to be done, and the worries were surely overblown—Phil often ate with competitors, and this was a trade show anyway.

When Hal came by to say hello, Phil shook his hand, then introduced us, and we shook too. Yes, the hand was big, and a good shake—but I couldn't get as passionate about it as Phil, who finds interest and excitement in so many things.

The euphoria of being selected by Phil to be the only bidder for his business was soon offset by some realities. *(Read **Don't Get Swept Away** at chapter's end.)* They were:

1. It had only been four months since our second deal closed. Operationally we were fully loaded.
2. The second deal had pushed us into being a net borrower. Our leverage wasn't high, but we preferred to have no bank debt.

3. Aaron Ashley sales were more than double our largest acquisition. Company revenues of past acquisitions had each been less than 10% of our size, but Ashley's was about 25%. His bottom line was strong as well, which would push up the selling price.

4. Phil had negotiated with other suitors a few years back to the point of getting a hard offer on the table, so he did have a benchmark of value.

5. Phil had two silent partners who might be looking over his shoulder. This wasn't just about Phil. *(Thinking carefully about all those that you need to persuade is important and is discussed in **Don't Forget the Spouse** at chapter's end.)*

6. Our rate of sales growth was declining, and in this quarter, sales to date were down over the same quarter a year prior, despite having a new acquisition bringing in 10% of total revenues! Something was wrong out there—we hadn't really changed what we did much (aside from two acquisitions), but it felt like demand had decreased. This was a big, nagging, serious worry. But over the years I have made many strategic moves when the business was having short-term headaches. Some of those moves helped us survive the short-term problems. Becoming frozen from fear in tough times is dangerous. Being prudent in your spending is good in tough times, but should not necessarily mean tossing out the pursuit of your long-term vision.

7. Our margins were positive but not robust right now.

8. Our cash flow was being taxed by payments to both sellers—which would continue for several more years. A big balloon payment was due in six months on the second deal.

   It has been interesting to see that many members of my team, upon learning that one of the things absorbing our cash is payments to sellers, feel like buying the companies was a bad thing. They forget that the larger sales every month are not only funding the payments but carrying a nice chunk of overhead as well. This has been true of the majority of people up and down the ranks. What information to share with team members, and how to share it about an acquisition, is a big issue—too big to tackle here.

Wouldn't it be great if all opportunities came along at the perfect time? But they often don't, and it's our job to deal with it. This opportunity was an excellent one, and even though I was worried about the timing, asking Phil to wait a few years wasn't the right answer.

Half of me was saying, "I've got to do this deal—go for it," and the other half was saying, "This is too much too fast—walk away from it." But neither impulse was right; they were both premature. Just as jumping into a price negotiation up front is always wrong, so too is jumping to conclusions.

As the entrées arrived I dove into both my steak and my journey to understand Phil's needs, wants, and desires relating to the sale of Aaron Ashley. For so many months, acquisition questions had been on hold in favor of making friends. The tables were now turned, and I peppered him with questions.

1. "Phil, what are you going to do after the sale? How much involvement would you like?"
2. "What about your staff? How do you feel about Henry in particular with 40+ years of service?"
3. "What about the Manhattan office, and your two warehouses? Are all of them needed in your opinion?"
4. "Do you want the real property (the warehouse) to be part of the sale?"
5. "What have your sales been, and what do you expect them to be?"
6. "How profitable has the firm been over time?"
7. "Why are you selling now?" (He had told me, but I wanted to really dig into this.)
8. "How do your partners feel about this? What will their role in the negotiations be?"
9. "What access to data/records will I have, and when?"
10. "In your organization, who knows about our discussions on this matter?"
11. "How do you feel we can best grow Aaron Ashley? What are its most valuable points?"
12. "What do you *not* want to see happen to Aaron Ashley after the sale?"
13. "What are you most worried about in this sale process? What are your concerns?"
14. "Lastly, what do you think it is worth, and what are your thoughts about the terms?"

If consuming this steak dinner was a contest, I was winning, with Phil answering all my questions. *(For each of the questions above, I had real reasons behind the questions, and a real goal I was trying to achieve. Read about my thinking at a much deeper level at chapter's end. **The Questioner's Quarry**.)*

Most of his answers were good and expected. I was getting a full-bodied picture of his state of mind and objectives. The price he put out: nine million dollars[1]— was full-bodied too. It was the price he was offered by several of the more affluent and acquisition-hungry competitors a few years back, when Ashley's sales were significantly higher. It was 8 to 10 times higher than the price we'd paid for each of our prior acquisitions, and frankly, it felt impossible. It did feel good that he had received and rejected five offers by big firms in our industry, and yet he was here, wanting to work with me. *(**Sometimes the Seller Just Isn't Ready to Sell!** Be warned at chapter's end.)*

I hoped the dismay I felt upon hearing that number was a little transparent. It never hurts to signal that the starting price in negotiations—and Phil had put it exactly that way—was unacceptably high. But no buyer wants to be thought of as unacceptably poor either, because that ends negotiations quickly.

It was Phil's turn to ask questions. He didn't have many. He wanted to know our net sales and was unimpressed. "I would have thought that your numbers were larger," he

---

[1] This number has been altered to protect confidentiality. The real number lies between 1 and 25 million

said. "Can you afford to buy Aaron Ashley?" I assured him we could, explaining that we'd need a payout schedule that allowed us to use some of the cash flow from Aaron Ashley sales to make the payments. I told him just enough to keep the negotiations going but not so much to make him think we had plenty of cash lying around. That wasn't hard, since it was true.

I explained that for us, an acquisition of this size was a very important decision, and I would need to dig deeply into Aaron Ashley's transactional records to analyze exactly what was happening under the hood. That included customer names, individual inventory items, and more. I assured him none of it would ever be used for competitive purposes. My purpose was to try and justify the price (which felt enormous) he was asking.

Phil pledged full support and told me he would hook me up with their IT consultant, who could export the records I needed. Phil kept no secrets from Aaron Ashley's general manager Henry Kuver, so he would be kept up to date by Phil. We also agreed to swap financial statements. The conversation shifted purposefully away from business as we started on our last drink, in preparation for the walk back to the Omni Hotel.

We both felt good having shared our thoughts and feelings about the potential acquisition. We'd not gotten to the point of hard negotiations. It would have been too soon. I didn't yet know enough to challenge his opinions of value. Buying a business can be a great shortcut to building one's business, but trying to shortcut the process of negotiating the purchase is never a good idea. Some things must be allowed to evolve.

I guided Phil back to his room at the Omni, then walked over to my room at the Holiday Inn. My head was churning with thoughts, ideas, and strategies. Sleep would not come soon.

I decided to write down what I'd learned, as I would soon need to begin sharing this with my board. If you'd like to see exactly what I wrote that night, jump to page 148 to read my notes.

Writing thoughts and facts down usually calms me. But the questions kept hammering away.

- Could it really be worth 9 million, or was he dreaming? I discovered later that this was effectively 11 times EBITDA, quite a high multiplier! But Phil never looked at it that way.
- Could we afford 9 million? Even over 4 years? (I started calculating in my head the monthly contribution margin, less the taxes, compared to the monthly payment due....)
- Would he take less? How much less?
- Sales were declining at Ashley. Why? Would they continue to decline?
- Sales had started to decline at my own firm. Unless we had some great orders all of a sudden, this quarter would end slightly down from a year ago, the first downturn in sales in about 2 years. Much of the sales growth in the past 15 months had stemmed from the acquisitions—not from our

"core" businesses. Why was this happening? If this continued, it would start draining cash and profits. Would it continue?

- Was his business—essentially homogenous to mine—a gold mine in some way that mine was not? If so, what was his secret?

Eventually, enough time in the horizontal position did its job, and I drifted off to sleep.

Rob's Reflections: Chapter 6

Don't Get Swept Away
Buying companies is exciting. Just like in house hunting, it's easy to get swept away by the excitement and forget to keep a level head. By training and by nature, I tend to look at both sides of every situation. Still, it was hard to offset excitement with caution. The best antidote for me is to funnel my energy into the search for facts—in acquisition parlance, due diligence. Of course it's also really important not to say "Yes" too fast. Take your time. If you're being rushed by the seller, beware.

Don't Forget the Spouse
Understanding who has to be convinced to close a deal is critical. If it's more than one person, craft a strategy to help influence all the decision makers. In this case, Phil was to be our only official contact. I do think, however, his wife Rachel's assessment of me was important too. Most spouses' opinions have a significant effect on decisions, even if they are not officially involved. So pay attention to the spouses. As it turned out, Phil's partners had given him full authority to make a deal. But I didn't know that at the time.

The Questioner's Quarry
I've detailed here the main questions I asked at the big dinner when Phil told me he had officially decided to sell. Under each question are the reasons why I asked them.

I asked, "Phil, what are you going to do after the sale? How much involvement would you like?"

> This is possibly the most important question in an acquisition such as this, since selling the business is a major life-changing event, and understanding if the seller has really come to terms with this is critical. Either way, helping the seller become comfortable with his new role in life is critical to closing the deal.

I asked, "What about your staff? How do you feel about Henry in particular (40+ years of service)?"

> Most sellers have some level of attachment to their staff. Understanding this guides the deal structure. The emotions on this topic do wear off fairly quickly, but often, sellers don't want to feel guilty for what happens to the team that has been loyal to them over the years. This is why many firms are sold to employees for a lot less than the market price.

I asked, "What about the Manhattan office, and your two warehouses? Are all of them needed in your opinion?"

> Longstanding businesses often do things because they've always done it that way, and changing is just too hard. Identifying

big things that can be stopped/changed to achieve big savings or improvements is key to understanding the value you could bring to an acquisition—and it helps you justify paying more if you have to.

I asked, "Do you want the real property (the warehouse) to be part of the sale?"

One of the fundamental steps in looking at an acquisition is understanding exactly what assets and liabilities are in the transaction. Many deals blow up way later in the process because of confusion about what parts and pieces are actually changing hands.

I asked, "What have your sales been, and what do you expect them to be? How profitable has the firm been over time?"

A fundamental question for figuring out their size and possible value ranges.

I asked, "Why are you selling now? (He had told me, but I wanted to really dig into this.) How do your partners feel about this? What will their role in the negotiations be?"

Selling a business is a big change, and there is always motivation behind the decision. Understanding the motivation is critical and should be an obsession. *An article that delves into the details of this, and lists many of the reasons sellers do sell can be found on page 212.*

I asked, "What access to data/records will I have, and when?"

> Much as I am a generally trusting guy, it's the buyer's duty to check everything out. Even with ethical sellers, some negative items are always withheld unless you ask about it point blank. Some are negative for you, but the seller has gotten used to them and forgets to mention them. Many are just different assumptions about what is normal or obvious. A big part of the story emerges only when you dig into data and documents.

I asked, "In your organization, who knows about our discussions on this matter?"

> The other big treasure trove of information lies in talking to people about the company. Employees are important, but so are suppliers, customers, and others. But this is more tricky than data, because sellers are worried about letting knowledge of an impending sale get out before the sale is actually consummated (because it might not be consummated). I asked because if some others knew, then I could talk to them earlier rather than later.

I asked, "How do you feel we can best grow Aaron Ashley? What are its most valuable points?"

> Never forget to ask the seller how to grow the business. Their advice is important. But the next question is why they never did it. And if they are attaching a big portion of the value of the business to the growth potential, you have an opportunity to attach a big portion of the price to an earn-out— payments to them conditioned on that growth being realized.

I asked, "What do you *not* want to see happen to Aaron Ashley after the sale?"

> Good to know, because if you accidentally suggest that one or more of these things will be happening, your price goes up or the seller may walk away.

I asked, "What are you most worried about in this sale process? What are your concerns?"

> Worried, afraid sellers often kill deals. If you can get them to be honest and really tell you the truth, you have a chance at calming those fears—either by force of personality, by deal structure, or through due diligence.

I asked, "Lastly, what do you think it is worth, and what are your thoughts about the terms?"

I always like them to go first. It establishes the ceiling. 50% of the time I have been surprised at how low the starting point was. But not this time.

Sometimes the Seller Just Isn't Ready to Sell!

One could conclude that Phil was incapable of selling his business. In fact, this is often the case. But from what he said, the reasons for not selling in the past were a combination of things. Mostly, the timing wasn't right for Phil. When some of the offers came in, he was "at his prime" and enjoying his business too much. In other cases, he hadn't fully trusted the suitors—not that they wouldn't pay what they had agreed, but that they wouldn't care about the company in the way that Phil did. Whatever I had done over the past few years to create that feeling of trust with Phil was worth a lot. If you keep reading, you'll learn just how much (in dollars).

Chapter 7: Just the Facts, Ma'am

This chapter is the mystery inside the story. Wading hip deep into the numbers may sound boring to the uninitiated, but in truth, it is a mission of discovery—to see the hidden truths (or hidden lies) deep inside a business.

Financial statements are really important. *Sometimes they are even accurate.* Tax returns are also important, and *more often* accurate. Remember that this is the world that exists below audited financial statements. *(**Cooked Books** at chapter's end talks about some of the bookkeeping issues you'll likely confront.)*

In this deal, just like my prior two deals, I was buying a competitor, essentially homogenous to our business, and my plan was to move the inventory into my facility and sell it as my own. So all the seller's overhead would be gone (replaced in some part by my own overhead increases). Even the production of the goods would be handled through our normal channels – and I knew what those costs were. *(**Does EBITDA Always Matter?** The answer is no, and I explain at chapter's end.)*

My greatest area of interest was in understanding the underlying details—such as the amount of each inventory item on hand and how each is selling, which customers are active, and how many new product introductions were made and how they sold. I also wanted to check the validity of the financial statements by adding up all the invoices and items myself.

*For my reasons on why going into this level of detail can be critical, read, **Put on Your Green Eye Shades** in chapter 14 on page 161. If you're a CEO doing acquisitions, this is a really important commentary to study.*

At times like this I love computers most. In the old days, to review this much data would take months, and truckloads of paperwork. But not anymore. Every accounting system I have found, sometimes with the help of a programmer, can export data files. Most databases for accounting systems are relational and have similar structures.

I wrote up my wish list of data, including the tables and the fields in those tables that I needed. I e-mailed it off to their programmer, and we had a 10-minute discussion.

It took the programmer about six hours to output this data, but as a contractor to Ashley, he had other clients to attend to. About 10 (agonizing) days later, the data files arrived in an e-mail. *(Why they shouldn't say, **The Data Is Not Available** is detailed at chapter's end).*

Month 37

Like a kid in a candy store, I dropped everything I could on my to-do list and dove into the project. Being eager for answers, I wanted to go straight to querying—which is a form of program to get answers to my questions. But having used Access since Microsoft first offered version 1.0, and having already done the process I am about to describe in both the earlier acquisitions, I knew that the first timesaving step was to clean the data.

If you really want to know my secrets for data mining in acquisitions, jump to page 176 and read all about it. I've shared it all.

By the end of that day, I was ready to start manipulating the data so its story would be told. I headed home to say hello to the family, then quickly stole off to my study where I remote controlled my office PC and began mining the data. I went at it steady until the wee hours of the morning, hardly feeling tired.

As I write this, I flash back and liken my process to one of my favorite childhood movies, *Chitty Chitty Bang Bang*. In the movie, the kids persuade their father to buy the car and it comes into his barn, where he begins to re-build it. The scene shows day and night passing, and he never emerges from the barn. Through the barn's windows, the sounds and light from his work emerge, and you can imagine the intense energy directed at the project and feel the mystery growing around what Chitty Chitty Bang Bang will look like, and even, in fact, if it will run at all.

Okay, I admit to being a business geek. I find the process of discovery through analyzing a business' numbers exciting and fun.

Some of the analysis I did as the night wore on was planned and for me is a standard operating procedure. But much of it is situational and stems from swimming around in the data and noticing things—then getting curious and digging in to investigate. It's why I don't like to delegate much of this to a computer person. While they might be better than I at the IT side of it, they would likely not have the business sense to know an interesting bit of data when it scrolled by on their screen.

It took two evenings—about 10 hours—to finish the job. I suppose they wondered at the office why I was yawning so much. But then, they are used to getting e-mails from me at odd times—really late at night or really early in the morning. I just can't do this kind of work while being interrupted or distracted. Doing it while at the office is hard, with e-mail, phones, and staff constantly demanding attention. Laptops can be great tools for leaving your main work location behind and finding a place to concentrate.

The third night was dedicated to summing up the incredible amount of data. I put it into a clear report that would empower the decision making about what Aaron Ashley was worth. For me, writing forces me to clarify my thoughts. It often shows me what I haven't done, or conclusions I've drawn that I can't yet support. I'm a big advocate of writing things down as you make big decisions, even if it's only for the benefit of the process of writing—not for outsiders to read.

As dawn came, I sat back with the feeling that I had extracted most of the information I needed from the data provided. Kind of like in the movie *The Matrix*, when Neo could finally read the "code" of the program that was controlling everyone's perception of the world. *(But Do*

You Know What You Don't Know? *Commentary at chapter's end.)*

I'd be needed at the office soon for day-to-day matters, and it was time to shift into the next phase of the acquisition: Our projected future together, assuming various scenarios of price, terms, and sales for both our company and the acquisition.

Rob's Reflections: Chapter 7

Cooked Books

There's always the urge to cook the books when running a small business. It exists in its strongest manifestation when the business is healthy and throwing off profits, which will be taxed. While most small businesses run some lifestyle through the business, it is still contrary to the tax rules. I'm a big proponent of running a business in a completely legal fashion. Playing with the books not only makes you vulnerable to getting caught, but it sets a terrible example for your employees as well as distorting real business performance.

When you're buying a business, the seller is motivated to tell you how much he "cheated" because he wants to re-cast the expenses lower, which increases the earnings of the business to show you why you should pay more. And you should pay more if the recast expenses do accurately reflect the true business performance. But if you see that the "cheating" was frequent and widespread, and if the seller seems to have no issues with having done it, be on the lookout for more cheating. Cheating that might affect the product or service, cheating that might mean unresolved safety hazards at the premises, or a boatload of other areas where cheating will hurt you, the buyer.

Chronic cheaters just can't or won't stop themselves. Be deeply suspicious about everything you are told, and nail it all down with documentation. If after the first admission of cheating (which helps the seller), you discover more un-admitted cheating (that hurts you), think about walking away. Most of us aren't devious enough thinkers to really catch every area in which a cheater might do his or her magic.

Does EBITDA Always Matter?
I really wasn't interested in Phil's EBITDA. I was interested in what my EBITDA would be after running his business. Since I'd know what the costs would be (since I was in the same line of business), I really needed to understand his revenue stream and the assets that would provide that revenue stream— in this case, the inventory. There were a few expenses (royalties) that I also needed to fully understand, as they tied to contracts I was buying.

The Data Is Not Available
Almost all the computer systems I have encountered have similar data structures. There really is not rocket science going on. If any seller told me that his business data files were not available, I would highly suspect that he just doesn't want to make them available. The likelihood that they are technically not available is so low that I'd have a big trust issue.

It is reasonable, however, that sellers want to protect this very vital data about their business, especially if the buyer is a competitor. If this due diligence is being done earlier in the process (as was true in the Aaron Ashley case), the seller may release customer data (for example) with only the customer code. The name and contact information for each customer would not be given out.

This still allows most of the due diligence to proceed but protects the anonymity of the customers. Once a letter of intent is signed, however, this information would be forthcoming so the due diligence can be completed while there is still time to bail out of the deal if significant problems are discovered.

But Do You Know What You Don't Know?

Understanding the data is really important. What is even more important, however, is to know what you don't know—that is, what data you are *missing* This sounds obvious, but many people either aren't able to identify what they don't know or don't take the time to figure it out. What you don't know is often what gets you in the end—when you discover it too late.

Chapter 8: Painting the Picture of the Future

What if? I remember way back in some spreadsheet program that lost out to Excel, there was actually a "What If" function. How cool! Too bad it actually still takes a human and some solid logic to get a good answer.

As much as I would argue that spreadsheets do not predict the future, if they are built properly, they are a great tool for showing what will happen as key variables are changed. And trust me; variables do change, often in surprising ways.

In went the 9-million purchase price Phil was asking for. I spread it over 4 years, as he offered. Into the stew went transition costs, sales forecasts, out-bound cash to pay for investment in new inventory, transitional salary for Phil, and on and on.

At times, it looked like a horrible deal. Then, as other variables dropped in, it looked good. One by one, I fine-tuned the variables, doing more homework on each one to become more certain of the forecast. I was focused on looking not just at profits, but at cash flow and return on investment. *(**Stay Calm!** will be your mantra as you see the spreadsheet go from horrible to great and back again with a few clicks. Read at chapter's end.)*

It became obvious pretty fast that a 9-million price wasn't going to work, no matter what I did. Thankfully, it was a starting point, not an ending point. Even though I'd known Phil for 3 years, I'd never negotiated with him. I couldn't be sure how he would react when I started telling him that he wasn't going to get what he wanted—if we even got that far. *(I highly recommend **Testing with a Tidbit** to learn big lessons with low risk. I'll explain at chapter's end.)*

I also didn't know if his advisors had found a buyer from outside the industry. The process was moving fairly quickly, and it's hard and slow to find buyers, so I was hopeful that we were the only option at this point. *(If you're about the money, **Auction It** is a must read at chapter's end).*

I decided to test Phil's comment that he would not accept any conditional payouts based on future business performance. It was the only way I could give him a path to getting something close to his asking price. I put in that 4.5 million would be guaranteed, and that additional payments would be made as a percentage of sales exceeding a certain threshold. I also pushed the payout to five years. *(**When Push Comes to Shove** at chapter's end talks about figuring out how to provide tolerable tradeoffs for sellers.)*

The forecasting work had taken about a week, and it was early October. I had called Phil a few times to ask specific questions to help me with the forecasting. As I saw that his asking price was out of reach, I began to think about how to present what might well be a disappointing counter offer.

Plopping the offer into an e-mail wasn't the answer. I decided that he had to learn of my concerns and issues first, and to digest them, so that he'd be ready for a much lower offer. I also hoped that he might provide some clues as to how to structure the offer in a way that would be most acceptable to him. *(I touch on the process of how sellers can get softened up in **Sacrificial Lamb** at chapter's end.)*

Rather than picking up the phone and degrading the business that Phil considered a gold mine (and it was a gold mine, so long as you didn't have to invest 9 million into it), I decided to present my worries to Phil and ask him if he had any guidance. ***(Please Help Me Understand** is an underused approach I explain at chapter's end.)*

We talked about how I had quantified the sales on the new releases, and how bad they were. I asked why, how he would have changed that for the future, and how much investment in new releases he would suggest making.

I inquired about the sales downtrend and asked what his forecast would be, and what he would do, if he continued to own Aaron Ashley, to turn it around.

I shared information about our poor third quarter (it was too early in the fourth quarter to get a good read).

In each conversation, he encouraged me to counter offer. I would respond that I was still working to justify his asking price, but falling short. I also told him that my board hadn't approved an offer yet, but that I'd be presenting my recommendation to them very soon.

All of that was true. I believe that if you can find a way to give the seller what they want, it all works better. Now they may have to wait a lot longer, or have some of it on a contingency, but it often helps to allow them in their head to feel good about the price they received.

The part about the board was true too. I had a 20% stake in the company, hardly a controlling interest. The board was generally happy with the first two acquisitions but nervous about personal guarantees on bank notes again. There had been lean times in the past when we owed the bank money—really lean times—and the anxiety had left its scar.

They of course knew about the discussion over time and were aware of Aaron Ashley. The excitement over the deal was shared by all five owners of the firm (which comprised the board), but the sticker price was a huge concern. I should add that it was five EQUAL owners. This is not the best ownership formula, and it increased my challenges over time. *But that in itself could be the subject of several books.*

I led the company with a firm hand, and generally the board would go along with me on most matters. Given my level of due diligence in the first two acquisitions, they had approved them easily. The Aaron Ashley deal was much riskier, largely due to its much larger size. I would have my work cut out for me at the board level.

I needed to finish up my report so that my board would have a fairly concise document to study. As one does research for an acquisition, so much information is absorbed, that it takes careful thinking about what an uninitiated person would need to know to understand the essential risks and benefits. I realized that I needed to talk about the "cast of characters" and the facilities. I added to what would become my report to the board. *(Jump to page 151 to read it word for word.)*

It was time to present this to my fellow owners, who comprised our board. I must admit, I often dream of running a company without a board of directors. I'd get to do anything I want, without justifying it to anyone. But I'm not entirely sure this dream would be fully blissful in reality. Good boards force CEOs to create full clarity around their strategic vision. Duties like writing a report about an acquisition, for example, aren't a waste of time. It forces the author to be thorough and crystal clear.

Even more, a good board won't get swept away by the enthusiasm of the moment, or the passion for doing the deal (in this case). With a skeptical eye, they balance the decision-making process.

Having a real (outside) board is almost always a good idea, even when you own the company outright. Of course, you get to choose the board, and who you choose should be based on their business experience, industry experience, and their ability to help you. Most likely, they'll be on one-year terms, so if you are the owner, you can always not reelect them the following year. Choose them carefully, and choose those you respect highly.

Treat them well, and they can really help your business. *You'll find a case study on just this topic on page 218.*

A few days after circulating my report, we met as a board. There was genuine interest from all parties but a lot of concern. This had been true also of the past two acquisitions, but I had gotten the green light in both cases fairly quickly. This time the price tag was several fold higher, we had less liquidity now, and we had taken on external debt. I knew it wouldn't be as easy.

After spirited discussion, some key concerns emerged. They revolved around ROI, the need to borrow more from the bank, the effect on the business if sales fell off, and other topics. *For a detailed discussion of these important financial issues and for my commentary, read the section in chapter 14 titled* **Put On Your Green Eye Shades** *on page 161.*

After a series of meetings, the board came to the position that the deal was worth pursuing, but that there was significant risk. Both the total offering price and the structure had to take that risk into account and leave us room to maneuver if expected sales didn't fully materialize or if there was an industry downturn. I agreed with that position, but worried that if we came with too low an offer, we'd lose the deal.

It's a hateful thought to lose a deal after you have so much time, effort and ego invested. It's even MORE hateful to lose your entire company because of an ill-advised acquisition. Of course, its never that clear, and most of the time, situations in business can get pretty bad and still be survivable, if you have the fortitude and know how to operate when the cards are against you. Fortunately (or unfortunately) I've survived business adversity a number of times, so while I really try to avoid tough times, sometimes the upside of a gutsy move is very attractive and worth enduring a tough patch to get there.

Rob's Reflections: Chapter 8

Stay Calm!

Beware of jumping to conclusions when analyzing data, and don't let anyone look over your shoulder while you construct the model—as they will definitely jump to conclusions. I find it easiest to build a model not worrying too much about the right numbers, then tune the numbers later. But it freaks people out if they look too early. Also, about a third of the time the numbers will look crazy; then I find some logic/mathematical/formula error that instantly rights the ship. That's another reason to keep the development part to yourself.

Testing with a Tidbit

With all the years I had to get to know Phil, I really should have found some excuse—any excuse --to do a bit of business with him. I call it a tidbit. Just enough to have to negotiate something with him to see what it was like. As it turned out, he was such a straight shooter that it wasn't a problem, but that's rare. The notion of testing relationships out with tidbits is a really good one. I do it with attorneys, doctors and business associates all the time. If the tidbit doesn't go well, I look for another person to "test." If the tidbit is successful, then when I really need them for a big, crucial project, I know who I am dealing with. Most people actually use this technique all the time in their personal lives. It's called dating, and is often used intensely before marriage (except on certain reality shows!)

Auction It

If you are a seller, and you want to sell your business for the *most* money, you MUST do your absolute best to find multiple buyers at the same time to create an auction—where they are vying with each other to buy your business. If you are a buyer, you want to be the chosen one without an auction, as I was. When the seller really wants you to be the buyer, for any number of reasons, you will pay less. It's not always all about the money.

When Push Comes to Shove

Every seller wants everything. But when push comes to shove, they want some things more than others. The buyer has to figure that out one way or another. If they want a certain amount of money as the "number" attached to the sale because their buddy got that much for his business, then find a way—with time, contingencies, or whatever to allow them to feel like they got that certain amount of money. If they need a chunk of change SOON (like for their around-the-world sailing trip)—then you can probably pay less if you get cash to them SOON. If you fail to understand that, you may end up paying gobs of extra money too late for their trip, but OK for their retirement.

Sacrificial Lamb

Setting realistic expectations is a critical phase. I've heard that many sellers reject the first buyer, since most sellers have unrealistic expectations about price. The first buyer is a sacrificial lamb in that they disappoint the seller, so the next buyer who makes a similar offer can meet or even possibly raise the seller's now downward adjusted, more reasonable expectations.

Please Help Me Understand

Don't worry about appearing weak when you ask for guidance and opinions. I get more respect for asking insightful, deep questions than I do for telling people how I see it. In the case of buying a business, sellers, who have been running the business for some time, really like to believe that they know something about their own business. A newcomer sauntering in and acting like a know-it-all is not a good strategy. If you do have to deliver a dose of reality that is unflattering to their business, do it carefully.

Chapter 9: Our First Offer

On October 11, after some back and forth, the board approved the following offer.

1. A fixed payment of half of what he had asked: 4.5 million, to be paid over five years (equal amounts each year) plus interest.

   It was aggressive to come in at 50% of his asking price. Yet given the difficult prospects for growth of this business, this was an appropriate price. Spreading the payments evenly over five years was aggressive as well, since that would mean that nearly all the payments for the business would come from the business itself. That's great for the buyer, but most sellers will see that the buyer is not putting any money out-of-pocket.

2. For each year that Aaron Ashley sales exceeded projections, we would pay 75% of sales 0 to 10% over target, 50% of sales between 10 and 20% over target, and 30% of sales between 20 and 30% over target. This "bonus" would be paid over the following year, and would end after five years. Essentially, he would get the lion's share of sales exceeding our written projections.

   My favorite way to pay a seller more than their business is worth is to make it conditioned on performance. I was trying to make up for the low guaranteed payments by being generous with the upside. The problem always is that sellers have precious little control over business performance once the business is sold. In this case, Phil would have some ongoing role in new product development—but that's hardly control.

3. Phil would have to consolidate his remote warehouse into his main warehouse, close his NYC offices prior to close, and cover those costs.

   Aaron Ashley was 3000 miles away from us. We wanted him to do the tidying up of all these locations. It's much cheaper and easier overall for a seller, on his own home turf, to do this. The seller knows what is where, and what to do with it in a consolidation situation. The transition period is hard enough without having to manage a consolidation on top of it.

4. Phil would get 25% of sales of every new image he brought to the table that was published, for one year from date of publishing. We wanted him energized to bring in the very best art he could find until we built relationships with the museums and his resources for new art.

   This is 5 times the normal percentage in this industry, but it was another way to keep Phil involved to allow us to learn his relationships with new product resources. Typically sellers lose interest quickly in their old business, so incentives are advised.

5. We would give him a 1-year lease on his Yonkers, NY warehouse, with two 1-year extensions, at

$12,000 per month. We needed to lock down this cost, lest we buy the business for a fair price and end up overpaying on the lease.

6. We would enter into a 2-year employment contract for Henry in NY, with 65% buyout option starting the second year. The salary would be somewhat reduced, for a total compensation package of $80,000.

We did not want to close the warehouse for a year after purchase. Henry was absolutely essential to keeping that warehouse running so far away. We also knew that Phil was sensitive about how Henry would be treated. We were pretty certain that one year of operating the Yonkers warehouse would be enough, but one never knows. This clause preserved an option for us but also gave hope that it could be two years of continued employment.

7. Phil would keep his receivables and his payables.

8. The offer would have to be contingent on bank approval. What a banker says he will do means nothing. Signed loan documents are what matters. Since we didn't have a letter of intent, we didn't want to put in a formal request to the bank yet. Our bank had become so big that our key contact was now really just a salesperson who couldn't commit the bank to anything. I wish it had been different at the time.

Frankly, I wasn't comfortable with the offer. In both my prior acquisitions, I was able to come much closer to the seller's position at the start. This one missed the target both in the overall amount and in the deal structure.

Sometimes CEOs must and should do things that aren't comfortable. In this case, Phil's starting point of 9 million was just way too high to justify. When somebody starts too high, that can mean that they expect a bargaining session. In such a case if you return with a fair number close to the target price, after satisfying their need to bargain, you'll end up too high if you want to close the deal.

My sense of Phil was that he was *not* a bargainer at heart and wasn't bound and determined to play that game. But I couldn't be sure. I also didn't think Phil would walk away in disgust after our first offer, which meant we would have time to take another crack at it.

I mulled over how to present the offer. While presenting it orally with a written backup was the softest method, I felt that I wanted to give Phil time to absorb the impact of the offer before speaking to me. My plan was to fax the offer to him, then follow up a day later with a phone call.

But each time I approached the fax machine, I got a bad feeling. I've learned over the years to listen to those feelings. So I gave it some time. In fact, I gave it overnight.

When I awoke, I decided that we needed to negotiate in person. I called Phil and told him that it was time to get together, and if he'd prefer, I'd catch a plane to New York. But he'd been talking about seeing our facility and decided to make the trip out. He agreed to call me back in a few days with the details.

As promised, he identified some dates about a month out that worked for me. He decided to come with Henry so he could see the facility and meet us all too. He told me that he would pay all his own costs, as he wanted no feelings of obligation.

Having already gotten approval for an offer yet having to wait a month for the next move, I thought about preparing for an in-person, multi-round negotiation. I had roughed out a spreadsheet that modeled how the deal would play out in financial terms over the upcoming 5 years. We had used it already.

I decided to intensify that model, increasing the number of inputs that could be quickly adjusted. I worked up inputs for the health of the main company, as well as for the acquisition as an incremental change.

I created two main sections for the model.

1. The main business (including the two acquisitions we already made).
2. Aaron Ashley adjusted as though we owned it.

Just as a book is broken up into chapters, then paragraphs, so too should be a financial model. The math should reflect the way an analyst (or a CEO) thinks through the problem. It's easier to understand and validate the results that way. *I've put the details of these two spreadsheet* *sections in the section called **Forecast Details**, on page 188.*

A forecast is so neat, so precise in appearance. The more you add rows and factors, the more precise it feels. Too bad reality isn't legally bound to follow forecasts. A well-built forecast is still critical, as you can vary your assumptions and see how change in certain variables will hurt you the most. Then you must plan to manage your biggest risks.

After some final tweaking, I was convinced that the model would quickly show the results of nearly all of the big assumptions we were making about the future. This is all you can expect from such a model. I decided that if we got pressed for price during Phil's visit (if we got pressed? Of course we'd be pressed for price!), I could project the numbers on the wall from my computer and let my board see it for themselves as we adjusted the assumptions.

When I earned my MBA, and in fact when I taught MBAs, we always talked about three scenarios—best case, expected, and worst case. It's a handy way of getting the point across, but in reality, with 10-20 variables, there are far more cases than three. And it can *always be worse* than the worst case.

I have found that "playing with the numbers" with a live spreadsheet gives me a better feel for the risks than just staring at three static spreadsheets. Doing this live with the board of directors that had to make the final decision seemed like a good plan.

After my model was perfected, and after taking some time to think things through and discuss the acquisition with my Chairman, I concluded that there wasn't much more to do without new data or further negotiations. I had a business to run, and I went about doing just that. *(Beware of Distractions at chapter's end is a note about minding your meat and potatoes.)*

I don't know what Phil did, but I dove back into trying to push our sales up. The market felt quite flat, and our numbers reflected it. This was one of those times I wished that this business were the type where you could create a quick surge in sales. But it wasn't.

As October's last day closed, we found ourselves 20% off from the prior October. I couldn't believe it. And to make matters worse, we were down 20% *despite* having bought a company (Levy) in April of 2000. So truthfully, we were down almost 30%, if we didn't count the new acquisition. This was depressing.

Depressing Financials

	3rd Qtr 2000	October, 2000
Sales*	-4%	-20%
Profits	Small Gain	Break Even
Debt to Equity***	.62	.66
Quick Ratio**	1.2	1.28
Event	Phil decides to sell	

*	This period compared to the same period last year. Sales numbers include sales from acquisitions after the deal was consummated.
**	Higher is better. Anything over 1.0 is good.
***	The higher the number, the more the debt.

Month 38

What a great time to be committing to millions of dollars of fixed payments to buy a business when your own business is in a deep slump! Had you been there, depending on when you asked me, I could have argued two opposing perspectives: That I had *guts* to be so bold, or that I was *nuts* to be so bold. I'm still not sure.

I brought up my guts or nuts dilemma at my monthly Alliance of Chief Executives meeting that month. (www.allianceofceos.com) This is a peer group of CEOs that I'd been with for nearly five years, and they had a good idea of my abilities and track record. Some of them ran larger and more complex businesses than I, but all of them had been through many challenges and were unafraid to speak their minds.

After I presented the situation, and about 30 minutes of Q and A, they were unable to find a major hole in my thinking. Some felt that I was biting off an awful lot, and that it could be tough duty making it work. But on the whole, they took the position that if I was confident on the fundamentals of both businesses, confident that this acquisition was strategically sound and a good long-term play, that I should do it, despite the short-term problems and obstacles. **Sometimes executing a long-term plan helps solve the short-term problem.**

It felt good to know that my Alliance group didn't think I was nuts, or that I was getting carried away by my ego. *(Having peers that can give you advice is an excellent tool. For a short essay detailing my thoughts on this, turn to page 225.)*

They didn't mean that I should ignore short-term problems. More revenues in any business with a contribution margin of 70%+ helps solve a lot of problems quickly. On the road I went for a week, visiting our larger customers in Florida. These sales trips (I tried to do one per month) were always productive. Customers seemed to like me and to tell me honestly what we were doing well or poorly. *(At chapter's end read **My CEO-Sales Approach**.)*

Just being on the front lines always feels invigorating to me, and I learn so much more this way than any other way. It's one thing to see a report about competitor activities. But the passion is stirred much more when you walk into a showroom and see your competitor's products outnumbering your own ten to one. (Even two to one sucks.) I'd always come back full of ideas and energy.

Rob's Reflections: Chapter 9

Beware of Distractions

Buying a business—or even attempting to do so—is a big distraction from your core business. Worse yet, it is fun, so it's easy to get sucked in. One must carefully manage how much time gets absorbed in the effort, lest the core business run amok without disciplined, consistent leadership.

My CEO-Sales Approach

The most common comment from customers during sales trips in the field was that they were amazed that the owner/CEO of a well-known firm would actually travel out and walk through their door. They compared me to many competitors who did not do the same. My approach was not that of a salesman, although my goal, or course, was sales related. My intent was to try to fully and deeply understand their business. We talked as CEO to CEO (or CEO to buyer) about their challenges, and what I knew about solving them. Sometimes it had to do with my product, but often it didn't. I'd always ask how we could improve our service and product as well. Most of the time I ended up talking about our products in the end, but it was never my lead in, and I never pushed. They all knew how to buy our product already, but if I warmed up the relationship, they'd buy more, and soon.

Chapter 10: Seller in Town

Everybody loves to give and receive tours of businesses, especially if they have something—anything more than offices. And a gloriously beautiful office makes for a nice tour too.

Gloriously beautiful wasn't exactly in the same galaxy as our offices. Customers almost never came to our offices, nor did artists. All of our "beauty" went into our products and our marketing. World headquarters, as it were, was in a concrete tilt-up building with no windows. The offices were plain at best, with function and efficiency clearly dominating aesthetics. The warehouse was large for our industry and heavily utilized. At least we had lots of art to choose from to put on the walls and offset the otherwise dreary offices.

What always made people love tours of our facility wasn't anything tangible, like forklifts, racks, or machinery. It was the buzz and the pace. Stand in a walkway for even a minute, and people would bustle by. The energy of activity was everywhere: Phones ringing, ad hoc meetings and discussions all around, packing stations working, merchandise rolling by on carts tended by pullers.

People who might have at first glance said, "THIS old warehouse is Bentley?" would, after a few minutes of feeling our energy, understand. They'd get that we hired people who valued what we do and how we do it much more than how fancy their desks were. Most people we worked with preferred it that way—our money and energy was focused on providing value rather than providing for a cushy work space. *(But **Plain, Drifting to Run-Down** is an easy slide. Read my thoughts at chapter's end.)*

I had really wanted Phil to feel our energy, so he would know that Bentley was much more than me. Of course, there was risk that giving him the tour would arouse talk of another acquisition. My team's fear that we would do it again was an issue. Rather than be eager to grow through acquisitions, they dreaded the difficult integration process, and my accounting department dreaded the more difficult cash flow as we faced making seller's note payments.

What the accounting team never really understood is that if we hadn't made the acquisitions, our sales would have been down even more, and we would have had tight cash flow anyway. But in addition, we would have been a smaller company, with less staff—probably including the accounting department. Both the first two deals were self-financing, except for the down payments, which took some time to see daylight.

Ultimately, I had decided that having Phil arrive at our offices by 3:00 pm would be ideal. He'd see the warehouse operational for up to an hour, as well as the office operations. But the team wouldn't see us locked in the conference room for long, private meetings. We'd do that Friday night or Saturday.

As luck would have it, the plane arrived late, and by the time Phil and Henry arrived, most of the team was gone.

The facility tour happened and only the skeleton of Bentley was visible. Phil was gracious, but I couldn't tell how much he really absorbed. Whether it was his bad eyesight, the lack of activity, or being tired from the all-day trip from New York to California, I didn't get much of a read. Maybe he felt the way I did: that what really matters is the people you deal with, much more so than the stuff in the warehouse.

We wound our way back to the conference room. I knew that Phil might be tired, but I had planned to have one round of negotiations that evening. Instead, I announced that we would just spend about 30 minutes getting acquainted (Phil had never met my partners/the board in any depth), then Phil would check in to the hotel, and one of my directors and I would take Phil and Henry out for a casual dinner. *(I Am Reckless with Agendas is a comment on how I use (or abuse) agendas, at chapter's end.)*

Negotiations would begin the following morning. My wife had volunteered to take Henry sightseeing in San Francisco, as he would not be in the negotiations.

As we sat in the conference room, Phil was charming, inquiring about the role each person played in the business, as well as about family and background. I kept quiet as everyone already knew me. Being intentionally quiet and letting things unfold without your strong presence guiding the way is an underutilized technique.

Phil tossed in a few tough questions now and then, just to see what the rest of the team knew and how they would react. It all went fine. All I was hoping for was that no one on my team would say anything that damaged the fine relationship and trust that I had already established. I also wanted my team to have a sense of Phil and his strength. It can be easy for a board who is not staring the other party in the face to issue directives to their CEO that just won't work in practice.

True of any time people get acquainted, part of the lesson is not what is said, but the observation of how people speak, what they look like, and the way they react to questions. People today really underestimate the value of face-to-face communication. Everyone (myself included) uses e-mail and other forms of written communication and not nearly enough two-way communication (like the old stand-by—the phone), or in-person communication. Driving to their office or stepping on the plane is time-consuming but very powerful.

Phil and Henry returned to their room at the Holiday Inn (just walking distance from our offices) and I wrapped up a few details at my desk. My director, who would accompany me to dinner, lived out of town, and was also staying at the Holiday Inn. At the appointed time, I made my way over and met Phil and Henry. We ate at a local steak house, but nothing fancy when compared to Morton's.

That night I didn't sleep well. The offer that had been authorized a month earlier would surely be rejected, and it bordered on being non-responsive to Phil's requests. I had pressed my Chairman for a second position that I could shift to on the fly, but his philosophy was to push it closer to the brink, and only have the board with the authority to adjust. I had to sit down with Phil and play with the cards I had. *(A **Gambit with an Edge** at chapter's end talks about brinksmanship.)*

When I was younger I'd spend lots of time rehearsing exactly how to say things, then make notes as to certain points to highlight. I'm sure it helped me. But after 15 years as a CEO, I'd learned to trust the blend of instinct and experience. I had an approach in mind, had thought deeply about it, and was as ready as I ever could be. I decided to meet with Phil in his hotel room and present the offer at about 9 am. I would bring his response to my board, who would be sitting in our offices just a city block away. This way I could rely on my relationship with Phil and could speak freely, without my board listening in. And there was no risk that my board would chime in and negotiate in a manner that might harm the outcome.

I could have chosen to present the offer as a *great* offer. But I didn't believe that it was, so that would have been a game and Phil would know it. If it wasn't judged a game, then I would have been judged stupid, since the numbers clearly didn't look like a good offer from Phil's stance, and since Phil had, as clear as day, outlined the kind of deal he wanted. The only other outcome to this approach would have been that I thought Phil was stupid and would not understand how poor the offer was, or that he might have forgotten about what he had said to me already.

I could have chosen to present the offer as the absolute limit of what we could afford. But since I knew the offer would not be accepted, it would be hard, after taking the

"I am too poor" position, to later reveal my gamesmanship and "find more money" to increase the offer. *(How Deep in the Doghouse at chapter's end delves into how long you should wait before becoming completely honest.)*

The truth was that it wasn't my offer, it was my board's offer, and I was embarrassed to present it. So my approach was to convey that very real feeling, and those realities.

I started abruptly after "good morning." I gripped a sheet with deal points on it just as you read on page 83.

"Phil, I've got an offer here for the business approved by the Board." I said. "Honestly, I'm not happy with it, and I don't think you will be at all. In part it's an assessment of Aaron Ashley, but more so, it's an assessment of our ability, without a doubt, no matter what happens in our industry, to pay you what we promise. I pushed hard to get to your 9 million..." but Phil put his hand up to stop me.

"Rob, no matter what your offer is," he said, "I won't throw you out of the room. I know you have the best of intentions, and I trust you. That doesn't mean I'll accept your offer if it doesn't meet my requirements. Perhaps we won't make a deal at all. But it'll be fine."

I was encouraged but not encouraged enough to blurt out the offer. I continued.

"We tried to find some creative ways to get the price up towards where you wanted it if all goes well for us and Aaron Ashley. We're happy to pay you your price if we can." Phil was quiet and waiting for the offer. It was time.

I laid it out, with some brief explanations. It took two minutes, tops. I didn't offer him the paper to read—he had heard it. *(**Listening While in Suspense** at chapter's end lays out my strategy for breaking through the mind-wall that suspense creates.)*

Silence fell. Men are supposed to be more comfortable with silence. But there are different kinds. Phil was taking some time to process the offer emotionally (intellectually it had been processed instantly, as I'd expected) and to fashion a response to me. I gave him that time and didn't make a peep. *Shutting up is an excellent, underused sales and negotiating technique.*

It seemed like an hour, but I'll bet it wasn't more than 15 seconds.

"I must say I am very disappointed," said Phil. He stopped, and his silence signaled that it was my turn to talk. I remembered this feeling from the first time I met him. *Unfortunately, the shutting-up technique can be used against you too!*

"Phil, it doesn't surprise me that you are disappointed. I know that our offer does not dovetail well with what you said you were looking for." I paused, just in case he wanted to speak, but I was out of luck. He let me continue.

"I worked very hard to justify to myself and to my board a 9-million fixed price. But I couldn't get there, no matter how hard I tried. I'm dealing not only with the uncertainties of your business, but with the uncertainties of our business too. I don't want to offer something that we are not going to be able to deliver."

I was trying to get aligned with Phil. I was trying to show him that I understood him and his position. If I could show him that I was with him, then I would have the credibility to start shifting his position toward mine. If I just hit him head on and told him that he was wrong, we'd just fight and cause damage to the relationship.

I stopped talking. That was enough of a monologue. I waited for him to speak. I didn't have to wait more than a second.

"The price you are committing to is too low, Rob, and I told you that I was not interested in any payments based on the performance of the business in the future," said Phil.

"I realize that," I replied. "But given that we were so far off of your target on the fixed payments, I thought that some path to getting more for the business was the least I could do."

"I appreciate the thought," Phil said, "but my partners and I won't have a stitch of control over the course of the business once we sell it. Frankly, we'd rather take less on a fixed basis than have to hope that the future will be bright for you. It's not to say that I don't have confidence in you, which I do, but I don't want to have to worry about how you run the business. Once you own it, it's yours." *(A discussion on this issue, **About Earn-outs,** is at chapter's end.)*

"That's true, and I understand," I said, "But as I debated this with my board, they asked me how I could commit to higher fixed payments when Aaron Ashley's recent releases had been so poor, and when overall sales at Ashley had been declining. They felt that hedging the bet with some conditional payments made sense. And there is some logic to that."

We both paused for a bit. We each respected each other, and it wasn't fun hammering away at each other's position. But business is business. Still, we were doing it in a gentlemanly manner.

I continued, "I hear that you don't like the idea of conditional payments. Just for the moment, let's assume it's all a fixed number. Is there a number that we need to hit to make this work? Any target I should push for?" In negotiating, it's best to avoid negotiating against oneself. It's always good to try and get a specific counter offer, and it moves their position towards yours, one step at a time. Until I heard another number from his mouth, the established range was between my offer—4.5 million—and 9 million. If he would have said, for example, 8 million, then the range would drop nicely. But my wish did not come true.

"I realize there are many factors," he said, "that influence what you are willing to pay for the business. I do respect that you can't and probably shouldn't pay more than you think it's worth, and certainly not commit to paying more than you can afford. But it's my job to get fair value for what we have. My best indicator of what we have is two offers I received, in writing, three years ago. One was for 9 million, and the other was for 10.2. Perhaps I was foolish for not taking them at the time, but I was having fun and doing well. While Aaron Ashley has not done quite as well in these past three years, the decline is only slight. I can't believe that the value has dropped that much. I find your offer overall, too low. You need to come up with your best offer."

Phil had not gone back to solicit new bids from the two people who had offered to buy three years earlier. Both suitors were in our industry and would have loved to make the purchase. But Phil liked me and liked the way we had kept the brands and market presence of each acquisition alive. After 75 years in business, the future of Aaron Ashley mattered to him, and he was obviously willing to forego some amount of price to see it in the right hands. The big question was how much.

Still not wanting to give up on the performance payments section of the offer I said, "Phil, as I said, we knew our offer for fixed payments would be a shock, and lower than your expectations. We're concerned about the performance of new releases, since the past few years new products have struggled, and since sales have trended down. But you seem very optimistic about Aaron

Ashley's ability to maintain strong sales levels and to find new art that will really sell. You asked, in our Atlanta meeting, to stay on for a time to help us make that happen. So we tried to give you a hefty upside if sales go well—as much as 75% of revenues. We're happy to pay you what you ask if things go well, and we'll be able to afford it. Frankly, we're worried that if things don't go well and we increase the fixed payments, we'll be draining our existing business to make the payments."

"Rob, I can't disagree with your logic," Phil replied. "I fully understand your position. But please, look at my situation. I sell you the business. I stick around to help you find art, and I will also give you every bit of knowledge that I have—and will counsel you in any way you ask. But I'm not in control. I can't make decisions. While I have the greatest respect for all of you, and while you've built a great business—bigger than what I've built, we both know there are a lot of reasons for a business to founder, and most of them would be your responsibility, not mine. I've been completely open with all the facts and figures. Our history and performance is what it is. The future is what *you* are betting on. We are talking here because I have decided *not* to bet on the future, so percentages, conditional payments and futures are not of interest to me."

Just like in our first meeting, he stopped talking and his jaw snapped shut, as did the doorway to the option of conditional payments. Picture Walter Matthau, and you'll be pretty close. He wasn't angry, just firm. I thought everybody in the hotel could hear that particular door slam shut, but I thought I'd rattle the doorknob just so I could assure my board that I had tried hard enough.

I said, "Phil, committing to larger payments in the event things went well—conditional payments was our main vehicle to get the total we could pay you closer to your target. What I'm hearing is that those kinds of payments are off the table." *(Why did I repeat back to him what he said? See **Paraphrasing** at chapter's end.)*

"You heard correctly," he replied. "I think you need to look at all those performance payments you offered me, and convert that value, such that it was, into a fixed amount. I realize that it will be less in total, but it's clearly worth something. If it's fixed, I can depend on it and it will mean something to me." *(**Give'Em What Counts** at chapter's end touches on giving what gets you the most benefit in a deal.)*

It was time to knock on another door. After all, the purpose of this meeting was to establish, in all areas of value exchange, what Phil's range of acceptance was. *(As the discussions develop, avoid putting out deal points that will never be accepted—that are outside the **Range of Acceptance**, at chapter's end.)*

I said, "Phil, when we met in Atlanta, you talked about a salary for you for a year or so while you assisted us in the transition. But in our last phone conversation, you pulled back from that. Please explain your thinking." *(See **Don't Guess** at chapter's end).*

"There are two issues." he said. "The first is that given your low offer, I wouldn't feel right about diverting some of it to me, leaving my partners with even less. I've had a great salary for many years, and they've left me alone to run the business without interference. Secondly, I'm not sure that I want the pressure to perform that I would place on myself if I were paid a salary. It's not that I'm tired, but I can't depend on my sight. So much of what I do is sight dependent—from looking at art to getting around the city. Reading is even difficult, as you know, and is only possible in short bursts, and with a huge magnifying glass. For both those reasons, please take anything you would have given me and divert it to the main offer. I require only $10,000 per month for three months during the transition."

I knew such a short salary commitment would give the board concern that he wouldn't be there to help us transition the business.

"Phil, let's assume we leave the warehouse in place and retain Henry to run it. And that we shift the day-to-day order-taking to our headquarters. What other things do you personally handle that we would have to take over? How would we learn those things?" *(I'm trying to get at the **Owner's Magic** issue here. An explanation is at chapter's end.)*

He went into some detail about tasks and responsibilities, but the heart of the question was not lost on him. He assured us that he cared about Aaron Ashley and that he wanted to see us succeed. He seemed sincere.

"Look, Rob," Phil said, "The offer you just put down isn't going to work. You need to go back to your board and do better. Tell them that I will not, under any circumstances, accept any contingent payments. Second, you can forego any consulting payments to me except for the three months, and lastly, I am flexible on the term, so if you need longer to pay, I will entertain that provided there is some level of security involved, and of course, interest."

With a "wrapping up" tone in his voice, he continued, "Rob, at the level you're offering, you are paying me nearly entirely from the cash flow generated by my business. That's great for you, but it's not much more that what I could do by continuing to run the business. What's more, if you're not willing to invest some of your own money in the deal, how do I know you're really committed to making it work? Aaron Ashley is a cash machine—a gold mine like I've told you. I think it's fair that you all put enough down and pay enough so that you're invested too."

It's too bad he was right. It would have been easier to try and show him why he was confused, and that we were in fact digging deeply into our pockets. But he would have seen through any dog-and-pony show I could dream up. It was time for me to turn tail and meet with my board. They had agreed that they'd be there and in place by 10 am. *(**Don't Wish for a Confused Seller** at chapter's end talks about how less sophisticated sellers are HARDER to work with and consummate a deal.)*

"Phil, you're right." I said. "It is time for me to walk over to the office and present the challenge you've laid before us. I'll try to be back in an hour." Off I went.

We had planned to reciprocate Phil's hospitality by having him over to the Chairman's home for lunch, which was large and affluent—sending a message of personal financial strength. I was smart enough to know that drinks were a mandatory ritual and had arranged for a bottle of Dewar's to be present.

I briefed the board on the negotiating session I'd just had, and we fell into discussions. Thankfully, everyone saw that the offer as we had made it wasn't going to do the job. There was also agreement that that business was worth more than the 4.5 million in fixed payments that we had offered. Our issues centered around the risks if the business continued a slow downward sales pattern, and how much new capital we'd have to put in to produce enough new art to make it grow.

We talked about relative investment. Every few months, we choose to invest money in new product for each of our brands. If Aaron Ashley was most likely to produce the *lowest* return on that investment, why should we ever invest in an Aaron Ashley piece? We even looked at the ROI on the entire deal, versus the ROI of new products introduced in our current brands. *(**It's All about Return on Investment** at chapter's end hammers home this fundamental point. It's not about closing a deal—it's about making money in business.)*

We also talked about the indirect benefits of acquiring Ashley. Our two acquisitions to date had put us on the path of offering a wider breadth of choices of art to our customers. Our customers liked the simplicity of dealing with fewer vendors and would often give "first shot" to those suppliers that arguably could supply most or all of a given job. Ashley gave us an immediate traditional line which, because of the slow ROI of each individual piece, would be costly to develop internally.

I cranked up the projector and laptop to model a worst-case scenario, where Ashley sales dropped 20% below current Ashley levels, to a low that had not been seen in recent years at all. We also decided that investment in new art, which had been low anyway in the past 24 months, would continue to be quite low—we would rely on the longevity of images that we all believed to be true from looking at the numbers.

As we poked at the forecast, shifting profitability, sales, and other variables around, it became clear that 6 million as a fixed purchase price spread over 5 years was the limit. It would be tight, and would require some borrowing at the start, but if things went any other way than really horrible, 6 million could work.

Nearly an hour had passed, and I saw the board becoming comfortable with the new offer. I too felt it was right but I didn't feel comfortable with any more than that. Although all of us on the board worked in the business, I was the one who saw the daily sales totals and had to make the hard decisions when the bills went past due. I was the one, many years ago, to receive the letter from the bank that they had pulled our loan. It had been one of the worst days of my life, and I had sat staring in shock at that letter for several hours before I snapped out of it and dove into a panicked scramble for options.

Just as I was ready to bring the board around to approving my next offer, someone said, "But didn't we have a terrible month last month?" We talked about being down 30%. The lackluster quarter before that came up next, and the first half of this month being down about 20%. *(Choose Where You Gaze at chapter's end talks about CEO mind control in tough times.)*

As I was lamenting the surge of negativity and worry, the large balloon payment on our second acquisitions, due in five months, was brought up, and the question about how we would pay for that if sales continued to be so poor and we had to pay for the Ashley acquisition at the same time.

What a bummer! It was all true, of course, and there were risks, and this was without doubt a gutsy move. But situations can be viewed from many perspectives, and this meeting had shifted to the negative before I had gotten my authorization to proceed. *(I hate it when I lose control of a meeting and it goes **Emotionally Negative**. My thoughts at chapter's end.)*

I fought back, reviewing how in the past there had been a series of short, inexplicable downturns for a month or two, followed by a recovery. I recounted prior difficult times and that I had managed to get through them, with spending limits, layoffs and other cost-cutting measures. I reminded them about the positive developments for us

110

as a brand as a result of the acquisitions, and the increased security we would have by offering a wider breadth of product. Lastly, I reminded them that our ability to cover our fixed costs (including our salaries) was dependent on our top line, and buying a business helped us grow larger, in part offsetting any overall decline. I heralded the nature of this opportunity, which once past, would never come again.

They heard me, and the mood shifted back to neutral. Ninety minutes had elapsed, and it was time for me to walk back over to the Holiday Inn and deliver our offer.

The Chairman wanted me to propose 5.5 million, in part to give us more room to maneuver if times got tough, and in part to put a number on the table that was short of our limit, so that Phil could get the gratification of, if he stomped loudly enough, getting us up to our limit of 6 million.

We all agreed that we should offer 5 years to pay off the seller's note.

Although Phil had taken our lowball offer well, I felt that multiple rounds of bargaining were not Phil's style (nor was it mine). He had asked us for our best offer, and I believed that he meant it. I argued hard that I should present the 6 million and then stand firm. If he demanded more, we'd walk away.

After 20 minutes of wrangling, we agreed to the 6 million as my last and final offer, but that the payments would have to start low and build over time, and that the down payment would be small. This gave us some breathing room in the event our sales continued to lag for the next few months.

The board motion was made and approved. To put the exclamation point on the "last and final offer" they all left our offices as I shuttled over to Phil's hotel. I wondered if this was what Henry Kissinger felt like as he shuttled from country to country.

An hour and forty-five minutes had passed since I left Phil. As he saw me enter, I know he must have figured out that I had fought a hard battle. I felt optimistic and shared my attitude with him.

"Phil, I've managed to get an offer that I think you are going to like," I said. "We'll commit to 6 million dollars."

"We've got a deal!" he replied, without leaving me even a second to continue, and reached out his hand for a shake that became a hug.

I was VERY glad for the reaction but hadn't expected it so fast. I hadn't had time to give him the proviso that we'd need five years and to back-end load the payments.

As soon as the moment passed, I said, "Please realize that we'll need five years to pay it, and we'll have to work out how we time the payments to give us maximum flexibility."

Phil said, "We'll work all that out. They are all minor points. We have a deal, and that's that." And he really meant it. I believed that he meant it, but I knew there were still dozens of ways that an acquisition could fall apart. Many of those gauntlets were still to come. However, it was clear to me that we were done negotiating for this trip. Phil had resolved in his mind that we had a deal, and to have pecked away at that conviction by talking about specifics would have been foolish. As I've written in several places already, deals happen in their own time. Pushing too fast just causes damage.

It was time for Phil and Henry to socialize with the Chairman at his home. A target time had been set for 3 pm. The afternoon had been planned without regard to whether we would have come to terms on the price or not. After all, if we hadn't closed that day, there might still have been the chance of closing later. Of course, it was much more comfortable having it all nailed down. Well, at least the price was nailed down.

My wife Renee came by the hotel to drop Henry off after sightseeing, and she and I went off, while the Chairman picked up Henry and Phil and took them to his home. We had thought it wise to give Phil and the Chairman, who were age peers, some time to create a relationship on their own. Age is a big deal. People of similar ages seem to feel comfortable and spend most of their time with others of the same age. I'm not saying that there aren't great relationships between people of different generations. I am saying that it is critical to think about the ages of all parties and identify ways to help all parties feel the most comfortable.

My wife and I, along with our other directors, met over at the Chairman's house at 6 pm for drinks, before going out for dinner.

As soon as the clock struck 6 and he saw we were all there, the chairman proposed a toast. Phil had been patient, because really, he could have justified having a drink sooner, since 3 in California was actually 6 in his time zone. He had much earlier seen the unopened, brand-new bottle of Dewar's in the house, and he guessed and confirmed that it was purchased in his honor.

As drinks were poured in preparation for the toast, he noticed the Chairman reaching for the bottle of Cutty Sark.

"You can't toast with me while drinking Cutty Sark," he said with some levity. "Please, try Dewar's—you'll love it." The Chairman went along. As nice words were said for the toast, we all lifted our glasses and drank. But the Chairman, who really likes Cutty Sark, took only the smallest taste of the Dewar's and suspiciously swished it in his mouth.

Phil roared with a smile, "It's not medicine!" Everybody laughed and continued. As Phil was distracted by a conversation, the Chairman quietly scuttled the glass of Dewar's in favor of Cutty Sark.

Dinner went well, and my wife Renee sat next to Phil. He seemed to enjoy her attention and told her story after story. Storytelling is a great way for everyone to have a great time. Most people like telling stories, and many enjoy hearing them. If you're ever stuck in a dying conversation, try telling a story or asking for one.

Sunday morning I met them at the hotel to bring them to the airport. Following breakfast, walking to the car with the luggage, Phil dropped back with me, a bit behind Henry. Then he turned and said,

"Rob, we have a deal. No worries about that. But I'm curious—was 6 million really your limit?"

Without hesitation I replied, "Absolutely. Anything more and we would have walked away."

"I thought so," he replied, feeling satisfied.

Rob's Reflections: Chapter 10

Plain, Drifting to Run-Down
Sometimes we carry this too far and under-invest in our facilities. If you're not naturally fussy about your surroundings, you can become numb to how they look to an outsider. Clutter can accumulate, paint can chip, and carpets can slowly get dirtier and dirtier. If cash is in short supply, it's always easier to justify spending on something that makes you profit, rather than spending it on facilities maintenance. Once it slips too far, it can seem impossible to afford to fix it all. Fancy surroundings or not-fancy surroundings both work just fine. But run-down or dirty facilities aren't good.

I Am Reckless with Agendas
Written agendas are good, and I use them at times. More often, I have an agenda just for me, which is a list of all the things I don't want to forget to tackle in the meeting. Don't forget, however, that an agenda is just a tool—when it makes sense, I may change or ignore the agenda if it is in the best interest of the meeting or the relationship.

A Gambit with an Edge
Brinksmanship is where you negotiate hard, right up to the point of losing all hope for settlement or an agreement, then, at the last minute, save the day with an offer that has the minimum concessions. This technique can be very effective and I have used it in selected circumstances. For me, those circumstances are when I don't care about having a

relationship with the other party going forward, and where normal, win-win negotiations can't work. I just find it's a small world, and the value of having a long string of people who want to work with you again, who feel fairly treated by you and who recommend you to others is worth much more than having some extra short-term dollars in your pocket. Perhaps I am delusional, but I think not. Even if I do have fewer dollars in my pocket when I die as a result of being "soft," the value of all those good relationships is worth more anyway.

How Deep in the Doghouse

How deep into the doghouse do you want to go? Oftentimes, when faced with a problem, you can choose to take the hit up front and tackle it honestly, or you can cover it up, ignore it, dodge it, or hide from it in some way. For me the litmus test is whether avoidance will put you deeper into the doghouse, even if the trip to the doghouse is later than it might be. You'll find a full essay on this subject on page 230.

Listening While in Suspense

When a person is waiting in suspense (like to hear their pay raise, or to hear an offer price) they often can't absorb other information until they've heard the part they are waiting for. I try to fairly quickly disclose the suspenseful part then dive into the rest. Giving them papers and documents can also be distracting from the message you are trying to give orally. Many people can't read and listen at the same time. Consider giving them the paper backup after you present the suspenseful news.

About Earn-Outs

The buyers of the world love to have low fixed prices for businesses they buy and shift large amounts of price to be based on future events. In "mergers and acquisitions (M&A)" lingo, this is called an earn-out. This is shifting risk to the seller, and the risk is substantial. For a full essay on this really important matter, please see page 235.

Paraphrasing

Paraphrasing in conversation—summing up what the other person said and playing it back to them—is a great, but underutilized tool in conversation. It gives the other party comfort in knowing that you understand their position and it allows the conversation to proceed. There are times when I am talking to someone while trying to make a point, and they keep replying, trying to make a different point, on what amounts to a different topic. To stop the madness, I'll paraphrase what they are saying, then ask them if they understood me, and if they say yes, I ask them to paraphrase what they understood from me so that I can be assured we have mutual understanding.

Give'Em What Counts

Offering something that the other side doesn't value is throwing money away. As the negotiating gets intense, test each facet of the deal to see what they really care about, and what matters less. The best

118

deal for you (and arguably the seller too) is where they get the most in the areas they want. Of course, the best of both worlds is if they highly value something that doesn't cost you much. Work really hard to find these areas and the cost of the deal goes down for you, and the benefit to them goes up.

Range of Acceptance

Establishing the range of acceptance is really important. Too many negotiations get derailed because negative "surprises" are introduced too late. Creativity in deal making is ALWAYS good, and last-minute creative solutions can be great POSITIVE surprises. But after a few rounds, you should understand in each deal component where the other side would say yes, and then try and pull those positions your way if possible. That being said, you don't want to tackle every point up front. Start with the main elements of the deal, and when those have come to terms, then dive into the next level of details. Once you've got agreement on the main points, both sides have a vested interest in closing and thus are better able to get through the smaller points.

Don't Guess

There is a lot to absorb and understand when buying a business. If you aren't certain that you understand an issue (and believe that your understanding is true) why keep struggling to figure it out? If something doesn't make sense to me, or surprises me, an alarm goes off in my head that won't shut off until I ask for the answer, or ask for the facts that prove the answer.

Owner's Magic

Every business owner brings some magic to the table. They have a number of roles they play that add real value. It can be hard to figure out the special contribution they make. Sometimes it is the culture, sometimes it's real technical knowledge. Sometimes it's relationships. But a big task of every buyer is to figure out who and how that magic will be continued. Having the ex-owner on good terms and motivated to keep the magic flowing while the buyer figures it out and executes plans is really important. Phil's larger-than-life personality probably meant relationships were a big part of the magic. But who could "be" Phil?

Don't Wish for a Confused Seller

Having a confused seller is actually NOT better. Confused (or inexperienced) people don't understand the truth of what you try to tell them, make mistakes often, and end up blaming everyone around them. They also take much more time to work with, and aren't nearly as much fun. In any business acquisition, litigation is always a risk. I prefer intelligent, experienced businesspeople on the other side.

It's All about Return on Investment

Comparing return on investment (ROI) between an acquisition versus other alternatives is essential. It's the bottom line for a growing business. Of course, you can compare two acquisitions that way, but you can also compare an acquisition to building something similar to the acquisition internally. You have to adjust for risk in both cases as well as adjusting for the time value of money—because building the business unit yourself will take longer. Even more so, compare the ROI of the acquisition to the ROI if you took the money and effort you are about to pour into the acquisition and instead, you poured it into your core business. Perhaps you could open up a new territory, or hire more salespeople, or buy that new big piece of equipment that would allow you to expand the scope of your services/products to your best customers. Make the alternatives you have compete for your money and time.

Choose Where You Gaze

As I wrote this book and researched actual financial statements from some five years earlier, I was almost shocked at how bad the numbers looked. Slowly, I remembered the emotions I'd felt at the time. Interestingly, I had pushed the "scary" memories away, but not the lessons. I wonder if most successful CEOs do the same. Running a company means making tough decisions and piloting the company firmly even when things are rough. I don't think I could keep doing it if I dwelled on and kept thinking about all the tough times. I choose instead to extract whatever lesson I can from the tough times and save that carefully, then forget the pain and worry that surrounded the lesson. I keep my eyes on today and the future.

Emotionally Negative

I could have controlled this meeting much better. Likely, I probably should have started with laying out the ugly news, discussing it, showing how I was taking that into account, and then shifted to the positives of the deal while diving into the spreadsheet. While surfacing objections (and the fact that the board mentioned the bad news was in effect an objection) at the start could hurt, especially if they might have never been mentioned at all, it guarantees that the emotions of the meeting will go from negative to positive, ending at (one would hope) a positive decision.

Chapter 11: Strike While It's Hot

Strike while the iron is hot. Within four days after his departure, I wrote up and forwarded an outline of our deal. It was critical to get well beyond the "six million, it's a deal" phase to something more concrete. With the advice of my advisor, I still kept it away from the lawyers—his and mine. I just wrote out the deal as simple bullet points. (*Having an experienced advisor is a really good idea. Buying and selling businesses is not a common event for most people, so there are usually huge gaps of knowledge. For more information on how to best use advisors, see my essay on this topic on page 239*)

- 6-million price
- Next was our proposal for payment terms. Since they hadn't been agreed to yet, we suggested a set that was favorable for us.
    - 20% in the first year, with less than half as the down, and the rest spread evenly over the first year.
    - 12% in the second year.
    - 18% in the third year.
    - 18% in the fourth year.
    - 18% in the fifth year.
    - 14% as a balloon payment at the end of five years.
- Interest at 3% UNDER prime.
- Three months' transition salary for Phil.
- A one-year contract with Henry, with an option for a second year.
- Sign deal by 12/31/00, take possession by 1/31/01.

- We rent the "174" warehouse at market rate.

We didn't even mention security on the seller's note. Why not let them bring it up?

I called Phil to be sure that he had arrived home safely, only to learn that his sister had just died. I still faxed the offer with apologies and encouragement not to read it if it wasn't the right time.

November slipped by before we knew it. What didn't slip by was that our sales revenues were still bad. Although November 2000 was technically down only 2% from the year prior, that number had the Levy acquisition revenues in it, so in truth, we were down about 12%. Worse yet, last year's November was really poor too, so we were well under breakeven.

Slumping Numbers Come in under Breakeven

	3rd Qtr 2000	October, 2000	November 2000
Sales*	-4%	-20%	-2%
Profits	Small Gain	Break Even	Small Loss
Debt to Equity***	.62	.66	.65
Quick Ratio**	1.2	1.28	1.18
Event			

*   This period compared to the same period last year. Sales numbers include sales from acquisitions after the deal was consummated.
**   Higher is better. Anything over 1.0 is good.
***   The higher the number, the more the debt.

The pattern of weak sales and anemic profits was growing worrisome. Beginning with our first acquisition, our total sales took a step up, but so did our total expenses, to where the profits from operations held constant. But as sales slumped, our spending stayed the same. We were in growth mode, having added a marketing person, increased our advertising spend (re-branding with all the acquisitions) and other growth activities. That, together with spending on integration expenses really worked only if the acquired company sales plus our sales added up to the right level.

In truth, the acquired company sales were doing fairly well, but the core product line was registering losses. Perhaps it could be attributed to lack of focus, but there was a shift of style afoot, and the decorative trends that had been powering our original company were declining in popularity.

The third quarter of 2000 had a small sales decline but was still profitable, if by a thin margin. The fourth-quarter decline, with two months in the bag, was much greater and was at a loss. Losses are bad any time, but we were becoming a net borrower with the acquisitions, and losses while leveraged are really bad.

Month 39

December historically is the worst month of the year for the industry. Most of the business is done in the first two weeks. The good news is that December is an easier mark to beat, since the total the year prior is likely to be low. The bad news is that even if you beat last year, the total is so low it's still hell on your cash flow in January. But sitting around worrying never does any good. I wasn't ready to slash the payroll and expenses yet, but I did feel like I should be sharpening the hatchet.

I also thought it was time to talk to my bank. Since we had what appeared to be a deal, I started the process of requesting an increase in the line of credit to cover the down payment and early cash flows. I decided that I should have a line a bit larger than I expected to need, since I could see the storm clouds gathering on the horizon.

I put together a fact sheet on the deal for the bank, clearly identifying what I was looking for. Bob, the banker with whom we'd had a relationship for some time, had finally gotten fed up with two consecutive buyouts and had moved to a small, regional bank, just like what our bank had been like when we started with them. Bob had been after us to switch over to his new bank, but to date, the old bank had been doing OK. Given what was at stake, I thought I'd give both banks the opportunity to get my business.

The first response was good from both. "It should be fine," and "I can't see any issues" came back. But I was seasoned enough to know that was salesman talk, not loan committee talk. The week before Christmas 2000 our current bank responded in earnest.

"No."

They would be interested in renewing the existing facilities but were not interested in any expansion. It wasn't that they had any worries about us in particular, but that headquarters had decided to adjust the portfolio of the bank in the aggregate and blah, blah, blah. No way to tell what was real, but it didn't matter. We would be moving banks now for sure.

With one bank out of the picture, that left only one bank in the running, and they hadn't formally said yes yet. Bob was saying "no problem"—which was better than having him say "no," but it hadn't formally passed through committee yet. The tension was beginning to build. I considered getting another bank or two into the running, but trying to make that happen the week before or after Christmas would be difficult if not impossible.

Dealing with banks is a real art form. It's critical to keep them informed about the business so they won't feel tricked or kept in the dark about the health of the business. On the flip side, telling them too much too soon risks scaring them off. *(For a case study on just this topic, please go to page 244.)*

As the business end of December wore down, it became apparent that we would be well under last year's sales. Having two consecutive quarters down pretty much wipes out the "random bad month" theory. The likelihood of a third bad quarter looms much larger. Defensive planning and cash conservation seem more and more prudent and are not easily fit into the same sentence (or mindset) as buying a company.

Yet buying Aaron Ashley felt, in my gut, like absolutely the right thing to do. No matter how much I questioned the logic, the economics, or our plan, the acquisition still seemed good, and I kept on it.

By December 20, the payout terms and interest had shifted in their favor, and we had reluctantly agreed.

- 6-million price was the same.
- Payment terms:
  - 20% shifted to 25% in the first year, with 40% of that down, interest only for three months, then the rest spread evenly over the first year.
  - 12% shifted to 20% in the second year.
  - 18% shifted to 20% in the third year.
  - 18% shifted to 20% in the fourth year.
  - 18% shifted to 15% in the fifth year.
  - 14% as a balloon payment shifted to zero.
- Interest at 3% UNDER prime shifted to a fixed 8%, which was over prime at the time.
- Three months' transition salary for Phil shifted to one month, with no specific requirements for duties for Phil.
- Henry's details stayed the same.
- The close and the taking of possession shifted to January 31, 2001.
- We rent the 174 warehouse at market rate, still undetermined.

My advisor was hip deep in drafting the "definitive documents," and Phil's advisors were looking at collateral and security. At this point, it was agreed that all the purchased assets would serve as first position collateral for four years, and we agreed to leave the inventory in place in Yonkers, where it would be easy to seize if we defaulted and they had to take over the business.

We also offered personal guarantees on the debt, up to $900,000 total (all five owners combined). We were going to make them drag the security out of us.

Phil's CPA (Jonathan) was on a conference call with Phil and me on Friday, December 22. He was completely unimpressed with our offers of security and demanded that we pledge substantial hard assets (meaning real estate or marketable securities) to Aaron Ashley. Phil was quiet, but his CPA was brash, aggressive and unyielding. I promised to talk to my board and see what could be done.

On the 30th, I wrote Phil a letter, detailing the efforts that I had gone through to try and be responsive to his CPA's request. I responded in writing so he could pass it to his CPA, who would be forced to read it. The CPA didn't seem like the kind of person who wanted to listen—he wanted to beat out of his opponent whatever he desired.

Not that what the CPA was asking for was unreasonable. Given the length of time we had to pay and our financial profile, the request was expected. But it wasn't in our best interests to tie up too much in this acquisition—one never knows for what one might need collateral down the road.

Here is the letter I faxed:

Saturday, December 30, 2000

Dear Phil,

In our last conversation with your CPA, he asked us to see if we would be willing to pledge hard assets (personal ones) to Aaron Ashley. My advisor explained the difference between a letter of credit, pledges, and personal guarantees. He also told us that granting a deed on a piece of real property was the form a pledge takes when real property was involved.

Since all my partners have been off and/or out of town since the 25th, I have called each partner several times to explain, and to explore their willingness to pledge assets. Until today, we have always been exactly equal partners in all respects.

At first my Texas based partner seemed willing to participate in a pledge. But after discussing it with his wife, he declined, as she is completely opposed to it.

Another partner, due to a difficult divorce some years ago, had drained her net worth, and that prevented her from participating in the [then robust] stock market. As a result, she feels she has insufficient assets to be comfortable pledging any of them.

Myself and two other partners (the Chairman and his wife) jointly own (1/3 interest each) a beautiful vacation home and we are willing to grant a limited first deed of trust (first lien) against this property.

Phil, we broke ground on this home in 1982 and it means a lot to us emotionally. My share of this property is separate property, not community property, so I am free to make this decision.

Partnership Issues: We have all agreed that the three of us should be compensated by the company in some way to offset the risk that we are taking on and that the other two partners are not. For the first time this will introduce a differential in how the partners are treated, and this will potentially open up a can of worms. We will use the services of our advisor and our CPA to help us negotiate the right internal solution, and hope that everyone sees it as fair. We are very mindful of partnership relationships, and need you to realize that Jonathan's demand for us to give such security has now pushed us into new, uncomfortable territory internally.

Here is how we would like to amend the security paragraph in the Terms Sheet:

Security:
- We will grant AA a first priority security position in acquired assets.
- The five owners of FAI will also provide their personal continuing joint and several guarantees to the extent of 27% of the purchase price. Provided that payments on the note are current, at the end of the fourth year (12/31/2004), this personal guarantee will end.
- We will grant a first deed of trust (first lien) in the amount of 10% of the purchase price against the vacation home. Provided that payments on the

131

note are current, at the end of the third year (12/31/2003) this lien shall be released.

Phil, we have maintained a total of 37% of the purchase price in security that Jonathan had requested. We have added the first deed, which is a huge and difficult step for us, but adds seriously to your level of security. We feel that after three years of performance on the note, and with only 35% left to be paid, it is fair and reasonable to release the lien on the real property, allowing us to go back to being equal partners. You would still have the personal guarantees for another year. And after four years of payments, and only 15% left to go, we don't feel any security is needed.

Let's get this deal done. I've worked really hard to get it to this point on the security issue, and frankly all five of us in the ownership group are running out of steam. This offer is responsive to Jonathan's demands and is fair to all parties. I've modified the Terms Sheet and have re-attached it in e-mails to all parties. As soon as we have a signed Terms Sheet, I will instruct my advisor to continue with the document preparation, and I will tell my management team, and the transition planning will commence.

I hope to hear from you soon.

Sincerely,

Robert Sher

There it was, fax transmission complete. The world had survived the year 2000, it was New Year's weekend, and the world would begin celebrating. I could too, if only I could have had temporary amnesia and forgotten about:

- December closing down 15% (before subtracting the newest acquisition);
- Still waiting to hear if our new bank was going to approve our request;
- A net loss on operations for the quarter;
- Security requests by Phil's CPA that we could not fulfill, and;
- A deal up in the air that if it closed, would add 6 million in debt to our company.

Slumping results hurts confidence!

	3rd Qtr 2000	October, 2000	November 2000	4th Qtr 2000
Sales*	-4%	-20%	-2%	-13%
Profits	Small Gain	Break Even	Small Loss	Small Loss
Debt to Equity***	.62	.66	.65	.88
Quick Ratio**	1.2	1.28	1.18	.92
Event				

*   This period compared to the same period last year. Sales numbers include sales from acquisitions after the deal was consummated.
**   Higher is better. Anything over 1.0 is good.
*** The higher the number, the more the debt.

Chapter 12: Attempted Murder

Month 40

Phil called back on January 2, 2001 and assured me that he would not let the deal die over the collateral issue, but that he would let his CPA continue to do his job. He asked me to keep the deal documents rolling, which I did. So Phil wasn't trying to murder the deal. The first set of docs went to New York on January 4 for review by Phil's lawyer and CPA.

Most of the business points were decided, but I allowed my advisor to communicate directly with Phil's lawyers to debate legal issues, wording in the documents and so on. Lawyers and advisors are among the most common deal murderers. My advisor wasn't a lawyer, understood the art of deal making, and since I had many years experience with him, I knew that he would follow my wishes and give me realistic feedback about situations in the documents as they arose. But Phil's lawyer was new to Phil, and certainly new to me.

With sales what they had been, I couldn't stay in the office. I just had to throw my efforts into sales, just as, over the years, I've dived into any department or area that needed help. This is a philosophy that I have held for many years. The role of a CEO in a small to medium sized business is not one of issuing aloof directives (not that this works in large businesses either). The CEO needs to be able to lend a hand and leadership to any department that finds itself lagging. *(For an essay on this topic, go to page 248.)*

The week of January 15, I was on the road in Alabama, seeing some large accounts. The nice thing about the South is that people (and my customers) are particularly nice and hospitable. The bad part is that the larger customers are geographically spread out, and it can take between two and six hours driving to go from one to another. That's a whole lot of time to think. I had a cell phone, but in 2001 in the middle of nowhere, cell coverage was dodgy.

I was nearly going crazy because of our uncertain banking arrangements. I had learned early in the week that the bank had supposedly approved the loan, but the documents had to be signed by two people, and the second signor was on vacation in Hawaii.

I wanted to believe that this was true. But I've learned the hard way that a loan is approved when EVERYONE has signed off, and it's *really* approved when it's funded. It was too late to approach another bank, and my frequency of calling the bank was starting to look like I was in a panic (never a good thing for a bank to perceive). It sure felt like the bank was trying to murder my deal.

Airline tickets had been booked for my trip to New York to sign the papers in two weeks. I felt like I was on a freight train headed into a brick wall. My board knew that the new bank had said yes, so they were not sweating it like I was. I chose to spare them the worry of knowing that the second signature had not found its way onto the loan documents yet. Honestly, I didn't tell them about the bank for fear that *they* would panic and try and murder my deal.

While I had been having fantasies during New Year's of our sales robustly rebounding in January (it's a new year after all), the reality had been abysmal. Deducting sales of the Levy brand—the last acquisition we had that hadn't happened yet as of last January, sales were down nearly 50%. It was uncanny, and all our customers kept assuring us that it wasn't us—they were all having a very slow January, and that our competitors were feeling the effects, just like us. Misery does love company, but it doesn't pay the bills. With more than 50% of January completed, there was no way that January sales could be good. It was only a question of how poor we would end the month. Poor sales were trying to murder my spirit.

Normally I sleep deeply, but not on this trip. I stopped by a drugstore and got some over-the-counter sleeping pills. On the long drives, I tried to focus my thoughts on two questions:

What are my options? What can we do differently NOW to improve the outcome?

I made a list. None of the items was pleasant. Each time I would pull up to a customer's facility, I'd stretch out my smile, take a deep breath, and walk in upbeat. After all, it was a chance to push the sales back up where they needed to be. It is actually an art to stay positive and sane when things start going really wrong. I suppose that makes me an artist, then, as I've had lots of practice. *(For my thoughts on this, go to page 251.)*

By the end of the week, the bank had confirmed that the hand capable of placing the second signature on the loan documents would be in the office on Monday, and the loan should fund by the end of the week. If that really happened, we'd have the funds three days before we needed them. What was I worrying about???

On the plane home, I thought through my priorities for the next week.

I'd need to tell my team about the deal, just as soon as I had confirmed that the bank was in place. Ten days for them to prepare was crazy, but it didn't seem smart to tell them if there was a significant chance the deal would die. The good news was that the existing Ashley warehouse, phone numbers and team were going to stay in place for a short while, and they could take orders after we owned the business just like they did the week before. Nonetheless, my team was still recovering from the work that the Rinehart and Levy deals had heaped upon them. They'd feel like murdering *me* when I told them about our biggest acquisition yet.

Next week I would also check with Phil's CPA to see what his stance was on security, since if we were to sign the deal when I traveled there in a week, the proper paperwork would have to be in order and there wasn't much time left. The CPA most assuredly did not want the deal to go through, and I was certain he regarded me as an unsuitable buyer. Aaron Ashley had been his firm's client since 1928. Today, Aaron Ashley was the smallest client for the firm—but the oldest. I don't know if this guy just didn't like me or just needed the deal to meet his own personal standards without regard for his client's wishes. The CPA was a deal murderer with a rifle *and* a scope. I wasn't sure that Phil would be able to jump in front of the gun in time to stop the CPA from committing the act.

Lastly, I would present an emergency cost-cutting plan to my team and then to my board to drastically cut expenses in February, since January sales had plummeted. So far, bad sales had generally gone from bad in one month to worse in the next. It was time to make adjustments, even if it meant murdering some of the momentum toward growth that I had been trying to ignite.

Monday morning I put on my "helmet" and went to work. I checked in with Phil's CPA, who had not backed off at all. He said straight out that he was not comfortable with the security arrangements and could not recommend them to Phil. We agreed that it would be an open item for our meeting the first of the week following, in New York. Of course, this is when we were supposed to sign the deal, and two days later we were supposed to take over. So it was absolutely crazy that all of these deal points were not resolved. At least it was crazy in my opinion.

But my advisor disagreed. He counseled me that very often a few key issues would come down to the last second, with high pressure to resolve them, and that he'd seen many deals pull through just like this. That sounded nice, but I didn't relax any. He assured me that he'd be available by phone and that whatever was decided could be drafted and e-mailed literally while we waited.

Monday afternoon good news came in from the bank. The plane had arrived from Hawaii, with the banker on it. He wasn't sick, hadn't been fired, the documents hadn't been lost, the loan committee hadn't changed its mind, and in fact they were fully executed. Funding the loan was on schedule. One less deal-assassin lurking. Hooray!

Before Monday ended, I held a company meeting and announced the acquisition. There was groaning, but much of it stopped when they learned that the Aaron Ashley warehouse was not rolling toward them on semi-trailers. I explained that we really needed additional revenue sources since sales had been down, and that this would really help us. I didn't explain about the 600K down payment or the debt load on the company. Hey, they needed good news.

I also didn't explain to the troops about the assassin-minded CPA who could still murder the deal.

The remainder of the week flew by. I tended to:

- Legal details: page after page of sale documents.
- Creating the addendums, listing everything we were purchasing—artists' contracts, lists of inventory and on and on.
- Planning how we would take orders in just ten days, and just as importantly, invoice them through our accounting system when the 2000 SKUs had not even been set up yet.

- Figuring out how to coordinate with our first-ever remote warehouse.
- Planning and getting ready to execute a sales and marketing campaign, including adjustments to a show already booked by both Ashley and Bentley in Europe.
- Watching the banking activities to be sure the loan really funded.
- Keeping close to Phil, the only person who could defend me against the CPA trying to murder the deal.
- Planning to slash expenses in a way that wouldn't ruin the business or the newly acquired Aaron Ashley.
- Doing whatever I normally did in the company when I wasn't trying to buy a company.

It was fortunate that I remembered to grab the $600,000 check as I dashed out the door in time to catch my plane.

Chapter 13: The Moment of Truth

I was lucky to get a reasonably priced flight without a Saturday night stay, so I took advantage of a Saturday with my wife and kids. As always, I snuck some work in early and late, but by and large, there wasn't much to do that was related to closing the deal. I opted for a late departure, landed at JFK at about 7 pm and went straight to the hotel. I met up with Phil at his place first thing Monday morning and went with him to his lawyer's offices.

Everything in Manhattan costs more, especially the lawyers and accountants. As it turned out, Phil spent five times as much as I did on advisors for the same deal. As Phil and I exited our cab and walked over to the downtown legal offices near 42nd and 6th for the final negotiation and hopeful signing of the deal, I could understand why these guys charge so much. The building was impressive, the offices were fancy and the real estate was worth a fortune.

If I had been another person, I might have been intimidated. Or I might have been impressed. But I was the guy with the unimpressive offices (to be kind) who looked on the trappings of success to be more waste than value.

I was coming into this negotiation in a great position. I was up against a wall, with almost nothing more to give. What the CPA really wanted was something that was off the table. I knew that Phil was committed to the deal, at least emotionally, and I didn't think that he had moved from that position. And he had said that he had to "let his advisors do their job"—had to let them satisfy their need to fight with me, otherwise they'd be angry with him. My skin was thick enough to take it, if it helped Phil.

We were escorted into a large conference room. The lawyer and an assistant were seated, and the CPA was standing, too impatient to sit. I entered as a friendly, relaxed guy with no animosity toward anyone. I made sure of that. Being relaxed, friendly and confident is toxic for everyone who is in a negative, angry space. It drives them nuts and makes them lose their calm.

The lawyers were calm and friendly, but a bit stiff. The CPA "sniper" was bristling in advance and struggled to be cordial. He seemed to be screaming inside. I'd sure hate to live inside his body. I wondered how much blood pressure medication he must be taking.

We sat down and brought my advisor, John Weld, on the line. He was always calm, like a wise old sage.

The CPA dove right in, reaching for the rifle and blasting away. The real property we offered was not marketable. His client would spend more money trying to sell it than what he would get. Our guarantees weren't worth much, since they were so hard to execute on. We were taking advantage of Phil, getting incredibly long terms on a price that was too low. John parried some of the blows, and I responded to others, sometimes talking about our history of honoring our commitments, and other times talking about our real concerns about granting deeds, or in some cases, our inability to do so.

Phil sat silently for about 20 minutes watching the battle. As he watched his CPA get more and more strident, he decided it was time to take control.

Phil turned toward both the CPA and his lawyer and spoke loudly and firmly. "Gentlemen, you are wrecking my deal. Stop it! It's my deal, and I want it. It's time to move this forward." Just like he had done to me twice, he stared at his advisors and his jaw snapped shut.

The CPA stood up in anger, walked over to the window overlooking Manhattan and didn't rejoin the meeting for some time. He was pissed at Phil.

The matter of collateral was quickly settled, with the personal guarantee winning in the end. The vacation home was deemed too "worthless" and thus was given up.

Document after document came out for signing. The paperwork was in beautiful folders, with perfectly made labels. I was guessing that Phil probably paid his lawyers about $100 per folder.

Then a surprise came. I was responsible for paying the sales tax on the deal, only about $3500. But noone had prompted me, and I hadn't brought a company check. That's when the CPA rejoined the party. He said, "Well, in order to close we must have ALL the money change hands that the documents call for" as he stared at me with distaste. The check for 600K wasn't enough to show good faith for this guy. I replied, "I'm sorry—I didn't know that would be required and didn't bring another check." The CPA continued staring at me, unyielding.

Then I remembered something. I always carry one blank personal check in my wallet for that once-every-two-year event where I MUST have a check. As I pulled out my wallet, I said, "Wait, I have a personal check. Would that work?" The CPA retorted, "We will gladly accept your personal check," and spun back around to stare out the window. I chuckled inside that a small-town CEO like me could boil the blood of this hotshot New York CPA so easily. It was check number 3140.

Now we had a deal. It was an exciting moment for me. It marked the climax of a 40-month process of courting and acquiring Aaron Ashley, and it was the largest acquisition for the company and for my career.

As Phil and I left the conference room we both felt great. Phil knew I was ready to fly into action to make the integration work, and he wouldn't have had it any other way. He took me to Grand Central Station, where I caught the train to Yonkers. Henry picked me up to review matters at 174 (the warehouse and offices) and to talk with him about operations as one company.

That night I took my newest employee Henry and his wife to dinner. They chose Nona Teresa, where their daughter Erica worked—her fiancé's father was the owner. It was a wonderful event, and later I had a happy, deep sleep, still glowing from the achievement of closing the deal.

My eyes popped open early in my Yonkers New York hotel on Tuesday, January 30, 2001. No caffeine necessary. I wasn't groggy. Just one night's sleep had shifted me from a self-congratulatory state to one full of anticipation and excitement. This Tuesday would be the start of something new—proving to myself, my team, and the world in general that the risk I'd taken would produce a commensurate reward. Henry had insisted on driving me to Kennedy airport, and practical distractions like getting through security, finding the right gate, finding my seat, and getting settled took up the next few hours.

Takeoff in a jet is always an amazing experience for me. Jumbo jets are clearly too heavy to fly, and certainly the contents are not meant to fly either. Yet with massive amounts of engineering smarts and incredible thrust, power, and speed, the jet rises above the tarmac. As the flight began, so too did my mind begin the process of making the Aaron Ashley deal a success.

The greatest successes usually rise out of beginnings that look ugly and scary. It's the "triumph over" that makes the success sweet and extraordinary. The CEO or entrepreneur's job is to find challenging situations he or she will have a unique ability to navigate, so that few others dare to follow. Success will be a big differentiator from all of the competitors—enough to allow for a big profit. I still groan, however, when I stare at the ugly and scary that I've carved out for myself from time to time.

While the plane was still in steep climb, my mind began to overflow with the constraints that would limit my options as I took the company forward. But I had planned ahead. I had put a blank pad of paper in the seat pocket in front of me, and so out it came and onto my lap, as tray tables were not yet an option.

A handwritten, bullet-point list emerged quickly, shadowed by a thousand thoughts.

- *Integrate Aaron Ashley into our operations. Huge job.*
- *Be able to pay the seller 5.4 million over the next five years.*
- *No more borrowing from the bank for a while. More debt than ever in past, at limit of bankability now. We had just had two consecutive quarters with decreased sales.*
- *The last quarter ended with a moderate loss. The last month (the first of the current quarter) had record **low** sales, the greatest one-month drop in sales (32%) I'd ever seen, and a loss. Must stop losses immediately.*
- *Cash tight as a bowstring.*
- *Big balloon payment due in three months to seller from second acquisition.*
- *Team is very tired from the first two acquisitions already. Must re-energize them for this one.*
- *Board of directors/partners are nervous.*

Next thing I knew, I heard, "May I help you?" "Yes, help would be great!" screamed though my head, then I realized the flight attendant was asking for my beverage order. Phil would never find out that I ordered a Diet Coke.

Being a CEO is not for the faint of heart. Month 41 would begin in just a few hours. Into the fire I ran.

THE END

Feeling curious?

*If you **really want** to know how the **company managed** through month 41 and the **difficult period** that followed, go to my website, **www.thefeelofthedeal.com** and **sign up** for my e-newsletter. I'll **send you** an epilogue that will summarize what we did, **how we fared** through the integration of Aaron Ashley, and **whether** we **made all** the **considerable payments** to Phil Ginsburg.*

Chapter 14: Details and Deep Analysis

Report to the Board, Part 1

(These details were first written after the Atlanta dinner, reported in chapter 6.)

September 13, 2000

Aaron Ashley ("AA") was founded in 1928 and is one of the oldest publishers of art prints. They specialize in museum reproductions that are largely traditional. Hand-colored etchings are also available. The images are not painted with trends in mind—they are traditional images that sell well over a span of many years. AA would be an excellent addition for us strategically, would fill in a missing product line, and would fit into our multi-brand strategy well.

The firm's hardbound catalog was last published in 1997 and is 410 pages. A 24-page supplement was published in January of 1999, and another supplement will be released in November 2000. They have offices in NYC and 14,000 SF of warehouse and back office operations in Yonkers, NY. No real estate would be included in the sale, unless we wanted to add it on. The Manhattan office would be closed prior to the sale, as it was only for Phil's benefit. Their customer base is very similar to ours, although not as large.

AA has had net sales ranging from 5.93 to 5.23[2] million annually from 1994 to 1999, with profit before

---

[2] These numbers have been altered to protect confidentiality.

tax of 24% in 1994, declining to 14% in 1999. YTD 2000, net sales are down 13% from 1999 (due at least in part to an industry-wide slowdown) and project to 4.7 million[3]. AA is an S Corp.

After introducing myself to the managing owner (Phil Ginsburg, now 73 yrs. old) in September of 1997, he suggested having dinner with him next time I was in NY. In March of 1998 we had a lunch in NY, and he broached the notion that firms in our industry seemed to be merging, and that larger firms seemed to have an edge over smaller ones. This opened the door. We subsequently had dinner twice a year, at the two major trade shows (Atlanta and NY). Until recently, he has not been in any rush to sell, and I did not push the issue. Phil owns 1/3 of the firm, along with two silent partners who have given him full authority to run the business and handle all aspects of the sale. The other owners are also the descendants of the founders of the firm. Phil was hired on about 45 years ago and earned ownership over the years.

In November of 1999, he had unsuccessful eye surgery on his only functioning eye, and as a result, can only see blurry, fuzzy images, and can only read slowly, with a large magnifying glass. It is unlikely that his eye will recover; the surgery to do so has the risk of destroying all his sight, and Phil is not ready to take that risk yet. I called him in early September 2000 to schedule our annual September dinner in Atlanta and to feel out his readiness, and he was ready to proceed with the sale, saying that his vision problems were the catalyst.

---

[3] This number has been altered for confidentiality.

He would like to have an ongoing salary/role with us for at least a few years going forward, much smaller than his present salary.

AA has had many interested buyers over the past years, including most all of the major publishers in our industry. Phil is a personal friend of many of them. The last "bid" was about three or four years ago, and was for 9^4 million from someone in the industry, and 10.2^5 million from an outsider. One of the reasons he turned them down is they would have immediately dismissed Henry. At our dinner in Atlanta Phil said that 9^6 million was the starting point for negotiations, and that he would not accept any deal that tied his payoff to sales or profits. He would accept payments over a four-year period (against the advice of his advisors). He also agreed to not solicit other bids from industry insiders, but would let his advisors look for buyers outside the industry. He considers his business to be a "gold mine" that has been exceptionally profitable and steady over the years."

---

[4] This number has been altered to protect confidentiality. The real number lies between 1 and 25 million.
[5] ditto
[6] ditto

Report to the Board, Part 2

(This section is an expansion of ideas in the comment on page 77)

Human Resources

<u>Owner and president</u>: Phil, 73 yrs. old. He will never relocate from NYC and seems to want a continuing part-time role in the business. Art sourcing is a big part of what he can and will do but also sees a consultative role for him inside BPG, using his years of experience as a guide. Also he has some key sales relationships which would be maintained, in particular with museums, and would look to more deeply partner with museums that act as both provider of imagery and buyer of posters. He currently has a salary of $120K, plus other benefits for a total comp package of $254,000 per year. He seeks a flat $100,000 per year salary (any benefits needed would be deducted from salary) for some number of years. He is wealthy, owns outright his 2500 S.F. NYC duplex, and is not hurting for cash flow. He would work from a home office (to be set up), or from the Yonkers warehouse.

<u>Operations manager</u>: Henry, 60 yrs. old. Has been an employee of AA for 40 years, manages the warehouse, accounting, customer service, trade shows—everything but not sales, not art selection, not printing. He also inputs all inventory receivers, makes collections calls, fills in for payables, and approves payables. He is in excellent health and does not want to retire. He has a strong work ethic and is sharp. He would agree to sign an employment agreement as needed. Phil is protective of Henry and turned some past offers down in part because they planned on

151

dismissing Henry. His current salary is $92,000 plus benefits, totaling a comp package of $170,291. The biggest parts of the "benefits" were a defined benefit plan ($34,000 per year for Henry) which ends 12/31/00, and whole life insurance ($27,000 per year for Henry) which becomes self-funding 12/31/00. Phil acknowledges that Henry is overpaid and that he would likely get a reduction in pay with the new owner. Phil may personally supplement Henry's pay, or compensate him in some other way upon sale. Henry is not an owner of the firm. Henry's two daughters still live with him (in their mid-twenties), and one is going to law school, costing the family quite a lot per year. His wife is a medical assistant, at her current post for 15 years, working for two internists. Phil says they are frugal and are financially secure.

<u>Designer and salesman</u>: Peter. With the firm about two years, Peter has worked for many other publishers over the past 10+ years. His salary is $64,000 per year, and total comp is $78,000 per year. He is personable, but his designs (posters) are of average-to-low quality. Phil has allowed and encouraged him to try and develop non-traditional imagery (like some competitors), and believes that there is real value in Peter. Yet much of that art is not selling and does not fit into the AA brand identity. Our current plans are to dismiss Peter.

<u>Sales director</u>: Ron. Ron left the firm in early 1999 after 17 years to pursue a new career. He was well known, did all the trade shows, and knew all the customers. He appeared "burnt out" and was passive in his role. $75,000 of his comp was still in the 1999

financials (plus defined benefit and life insurance), $91,000 in 1998 (full year).

<u>Bookkeeper</u>: Joe. Works in Yonkers. A 20-year employee. Would be dismissed immediately after sale. Total package: $56,196. Tasks were payroll (no outside service), G/L, general bookkeeping, payables.

<u>Administrative Asst</u>: Elaine. Works in Yonkers. A 4-year employee. Would be dismissed after two to three months of transition. Total comp $30,000. Handles billing, credit memos, order entry, order tracking, answers Yonkers telephone (customers have this number, as well as the NYC number), and types correspondence.

<u>Shipper/packer</u>: Robert. Works in Yonkers. A 20-year veteran. Would be retained until facility is closed. $38,500 total compensation package.

<u>Shipper/packer</u>: Jaime. Works in Yonkers. A 1-year employee. Would be retained until facility is closed. If he leaves or is dismissed, he would be replaced. Total comp package: $17,100.

<u>Shipper/packer</u>: Robert S. 8 years. Worked in Yonkers. Left earlier in 2000, and due to slower sales is not being replaced (Henry's decision). Package (in 1999 financials) $31,000.

<u>NYC office secretary</u>: Axia. 5 years. Speaks Spanish, a big plus. Would be dismissed within a month of transition.

153

Facilities

NYC showroom. This facility is rarely used as a showroom anymore and is where Phil, Peter and Axia work every day. The five-year lease has just expired ($28,000 per year), and a month-to-month tenancy has taken its place. The new annual rent is $40,000 per year. Phil acknowledges that this office is no longer needed and recommends closing it upon sale. I concur.

Yonkers "174" warehouse. This is the main warehouse and shipping facility. AA owns the building, but this asset is NOT part of the sale of the company. It is a 10,000-S.F. facility with 12-foot ceilings. It is mostly full, but more could be packed into it, and is all the business needs to function. Much of what fills it is obsolete inventory. The plan is to rent this from Phil, and the market rate is about $50,000 to $60,000 per year rent.

Yonkers "outside warehouse." This 4,000-S.F. facility is on the other side of town, and is a rented space in a public storage building. $875 per month rent ($10,500/yr). No personnel work there. It is not filled, and about 2/3 of the stock there is over ten years old and is rarely needed. The remainder is stock from an "acquisition" about 18 months ago. The plan is to dump all obsolete inventories at this facility and move that which has value to 174. This may require dumping some obsolete inventory at 174 to make room. This would be accomplished within a few months of acquisition, or perhaps during the slow month of December, even if before the actual sale.

Contract and Artists

The agreements tend to be one-page contracts and are simple and straightforward. When buying rights, Phil has always preferred to pay up front and own the reproduction rights without the need to pay royalties.

Judy S. AA's top artist earns 10% of net sales and gets 12 copies free per new print. According to Phil, she routinely agrees to forgo royalties on closeout sales. She will paint whatever Phil asks and has a great, friendly relationship with Phil. Judy is about 73 yrs. old.

Hedgerow House. This firm sells museum-type folk art. This company sold to AA in 1998, and AA will pay Hedgerow House 20% royalty for ten years, at which point no more revenues are paid to AA. This is a quick summary of hearsay about this deal. The contract has not been reviewed yet. In the late 1980s an earlier "Hedgerow" deal was done with some of the stock, and this deal is nearly over.

Hedgerow House sales for 2000 are anticipated to be $60,000, with 375 SKUs selling something. Hedgerow House sales for 1999 were $102,000, with 432 SKUs selling something. The best-selling item in this collection brought in $2,657 in revenues in this year. These figures are included in the total AA sales in this report.

Examples of other per-piece contracts are:

James Smith Fine Art agreement was reviewed for rights to an 1899 painting by Frost. Terms were a flat

$500 fee, 5 prints free in exchange for a 10-year exclusive.

Eastmoreville Museum of Art for a Winslow Homer painting had no price noted, no royalty noted, 100 free prints, and permanent exclusive rights for poster reproduction. It also cited a 50/50 split on fees from "special projects," presumably licensing projects.
Phil says he typically pays $400 to $500 flat fee for rights. More contracts need to be reviewed.

I thought it prudent to be clear on exactly what assets we would buy. A classic mistake in buying and selling businesses is making assumptions about what is in the sale and what is not. I encourage lists of both and being as comprehensive as possible. Leave no room for assumptions.

The idea of buying the stock of such an old company was not at the top of our list. I wrote,

Assets/liabilities to be purchased:
BPG would buy:
- Inventory
- Artists' contracts/intellectual property rights
- A/R
- Equipment
- Customer list
- BPG would also accept sellers A/P (typically quite low).

Not purchased:
BPG would **not** buy the real estate (174, in Yonkers).
Bentley would NOT buy the cash.

The hardest part is to commit to a forecast of the future. That is hard even without making an acquisition. I wrote,

Projections:

I believe that sales for 2001 will be 4.95 million. This assumes that the market slump doesn't worsen but doesn't get better either, and that some growth is possible. Based on detailed review of AA financials and expenditures, and with the anticipated changes, AA can deliver a pre-tax contribution margin of 42% while the warehouse is in Yonkers, and in year three, after the warehouse has been moved, a 50% contribution margin. This assumes $330,000 per year in catalog expenditures, and no price increase.

After considering all variables, including financing costs, moving costs, income taxes, a price increase, and expected costs of doing business, AA should contribute the following after-tax cash stream which could be used to pay the seller. This assumes a static inventory value.

Net Cash Contribution
2001	$1,917,999
2002	$1,723,599
2003	$1,469,697
2004	$2,166,381
2005	$2,267,895

With new tax laws, the IRS requires the seller to pay all capital gains on sale of a business in year one. AA has a basis of about three million dollars. Assuming a 20% Federal capital gains rate and a NY rate of 9%, the sellers of AA will have to pay $1,740,000 in capital gains at the end of 2001. It is assumed that payments from BPG to seller must exceed this in 2001.

The Affordability Question:

It would be a stretch for us to pay $9,000,000 to buy any business. Presently, we are borrowing from the bank. It has been six months since our last acquisition and ten months since we were out of our line of credit. Sales have been sluggish, and while profits are still there, cash flow has been slipping slightly. Attached (to my board report, but not included in this book) is our quarterly financial statistics that show liquidity over time, as well as debt to equity numbers.

If we did the deal, we would owe an additional $9,000,000, bringing our debt to equity ratio near an upper limit.

To have sufficient cash to pay Phil $9,000,000 and run the business, the existing business would have to grow sales at 3 to 5% (excluding the acquisition) and pull in pre-tax profits of 6%. This would be a challenge, given our past performance and the current industry slump. It would mean running the whole business conservatively and making sure not to build inventory levels—a traditional problem area for us. The business we are buying would have to run lean, and hold sales steady or grow, and *all* its free cash flow would be the primary repayment vehicle for 4.5 years.

I have modeled this, and the medium case shows repayment of the loan borrowed for the down payment repaid within a year, then a self-funding payout thereafter. This assumes modest capital spending and no new acquisitions for some time.

I estimate our borrowing capacity is just enough to cover the down payment but not much more. Of course, we are all on personal guarantees to the bank.

The current plan (as of 10/13/00) is to invite Phil and Henry to California to see our facility and meet everyone. Then to present them with some of the weaknesses we have found and propose a lower price, along with an upside if the business does well.

No such report to the board would be complete without a list and discussion of the key risks. I wrote,

Key Concerns:

New art chosen by Aaron Ashley has done VERY poorly (and we are not surprised, having looked at it). Does Phil still have the right connections to get good museum art? Can he supply us with what we need? Sales of his core line are declining (setting aside his new releases since 1998 and his Hedgerow acquisition). If we don't "shotgun" print everything new that is found, will his sales from new product be even smaller, and will total sales decline for AA?

What if BPG sales decline? What if inventory investment needs to grow? Will we have sufficient cash? Will BPG have to add staff to handle the increased volume? Another salesperson? Another accounting person?

The forecast assumes that Phil and Henry leave after two years. Is this valid?

Is Judy S. (top artist) healthy and productive?

Rob's Reflections: Board Report

Almost Always Worse Than Plan
Acquisitions almost always turn out worse than the plan. So make your "best estimate" plan, then be sure you'll be OK if it actually produces less and costs more. If I'm wrong about this with your deal, and you accidentally end up extra-rich with too much cash on your hands, call me and I will help you resolve your problem.

Financial Performance Tracking
In late 1996 I joined a peer group called the Alliance of Chief Executives. Part of what that group did was force each other to create some very succinct financial measures that were reported each quarter in our meeting. By the time the Ashley deal came around, I had four years (16 quarters) nicely laid out. Most of what I tracked were pretty standard ratios and numbers, but the last three were special for my business. By the time this book was written, I had over 10 years' data on one page. I tracked Net Sales, Q/Q Sales Growth, COGS %, Expenses, Operating Profits, Current Ratio, Quick Ratio, Debt to Equity, Sales/Employee, and three industry specific ratios related to the success of new artists.

Put On Your Green Eye Shades

(This section offers more commentary from the ideas on page 69.)

Reluctantly, I moved the deepest financial analysis out of the body of the book to the position here, toward the back. I was reluctant because the financial analysis of an acquisition is so incredibly critical, and no CEO reading this book should ignore the details that make a deal worth doing. I went along with the suggestion (by my editor and many others) because they know, as do I, that it's hard to go from reading an exciting story to cranking through numbers.

But here you are, which is a good sign. It means you realize that by looking at the numbers you can learn volumes about a business—often as much or more than the seller will tell you. The truth is that the seller knows SO MUCH more than you about their business. They know the weak spots, the hidden flaws, and the problems. They really don't want to tell you about them all. You have to uncover enough of the facts to be able to ask very pointed questions. If you do it well, you won't have many nasty surprises of consequence after you invest.

This section will blend what I did in the Aaron Ashley acquisition with my advice to you.

Digging Into the Data Feed

Early in the process you'll typically get pre-summarized financials and data. But typically, after the letter of intent, you have the right to get as detailed as is practical to fully understand what you are buying. In the body of the book, I talked about how I asked the seller's programmer to export massive amounts of historical data, which I analyzed with a database program. Below are some of the key areas I delved into in the case of Aaron Ashley.

The Data I Asked For

I wrote up my wish list of data, including the tables, and the fields in those tables that I needed. I e-mailed it off to their programmer, and we had a 10-minute discussion.

I asked for:
1. The customer table, listing every customer they had ever entered. (There were 6200 records.)
2. The inventory table, with stock number, description, quantity on hand, etc. (It showed 2994 items.)
3. The invoice detail transaction table—which lists every line of every invoice they sent out, with customer noted. (There were 100,894 records— they kept only the prior year's details on disk, so I had 20 months to work with.)

If I had been planning to buy their receivables or assume their payables, I'd have needed information in these areas too.

I explain in detail in the next chapter how I used all this data and my techniques for slicing and dicing it.

Non-Audited Financial Statements

Typically small-to-medium-sized businesses have either internally generated statements or their accountants have done a compilation or review of the financials—both a far cry from a real, independent audit. While you need to analyze what they give you, you also have to try and make a determination about whether the numbers in the financial statements are accurate. Sometimes they are, sometimes the bookkeeping is such a mess that they are inaccurate, sometimes the financials are manipulated to avoid taxes, and sometimes they are intentionally "cooked" just for you.

The more you become convinced that the books are "cooked," the more I encourage you to walk away. You could hire forensic accountants to try and figure it all out, but a good "crook" can always cause you serious damage, and you'll never know what you are actually buying. Go buy some other business in whom you have some level of trust.

In the Ashley acquisition, I had no such premonitions. The financials seemed reasonable. My greatest area of interest was in understanding the underlying details—things like the amount of each inventory item on hand, and how each is selling, which customers were active and how many new product introductions were made and how they sold. I also wanted to check the validity of the financial statements by adding up all the invoices and line items myself.

Inventory

I wanted to assess the value of each inventory item, item by item, because inventory turnover—a critical perspective on valuing inventory—really delivers its value one item at a time, not in an aggregate as shown on the balance sheet.

In my entire MBA and all the business analysis I've seen, everyone always treats inventory like a homogenous pile of things, but it usually isn't. What counts is understanding exactly which widgets will sell in the next period, and which widgets you'll get to keep for a long time, or forever.

Here's an example: A company has 2000 SKUs. 1000 of them sell quickly and get re-stocked every month—they turn twelve times per year. The other 1000 sell slowly, and with high minimum order quantities from their vendor. These only turn twice per year. In the aggregate, the average turnover is more than six times per year (making a few assumptions). That's good for many businesses. But if we could, after buying the company, sell off the 1000 slow items and be done with them, we'd improve our ROI substantially. Alternatively, if the business plan is to triple the slow-item category of product after we buy in, it would really hurt. My point: Don't be surprised by this, so dig into inventory details.

Selling History of Items

Aaron Ashley claimed to have perennial best sellers, immune to decorative trends. I wanted to prove that to myself. I also wanted to see if they had sufficient inventory of top sellers to carry us forward for a reasonable time—or if immediate production on many items would have to be paid for in addition to the company itself.

Sellers of businesses tend to stop spending money on anything that won't put money in their pockets. So maintenance gets postponed, new fixed assets don't get purchased, even if they are needed, and inventory is allowed to run as low as possible. Be well advised to look into this during due diligence. An overall infrastructure check is a good idea—there may be some really old fixed assets that have survived but will quickly have to be replaced, on your nickel.

As top-selling products are identified, the most important question is why they are top sellers and how repeatable that is. Conversely, you must look at the opposite—products introduced in the past few years that have sold poorly—and try to understand what happened, and if failures are predictable enough to be minimized in the future. In many cases, conversations with the seller are needed to come to conclusions, but the seller's conclusions must fit the facts found in the data. If you can't understand the success or failure of products at this level, beware of buying the business.

Customer Base

If Aaron Ashley were in an industry new to us, much more due diligence would have to be put into understanding the customer base and its value over time.

165

In my case, we already knew most of the key customers. Even so, as we reviewed the list in detail, we discovered some large customers we never sold to—a potential big value given all the other product we had to offer them. But upon close review, most of them were museums, buying only those posters depicting originals that they had on display. The likelihood of selling them any other images was low.

Finding and selling to new customers is one of the most difficult and costly things a business can do. When you buy a business, the customers come with it—at least at the start. It is a great "in" and is at the heart of making acquisitions a shortcut to growth. I say they come with it at the start because you must prove that you, the new owner, will treat them at least as well as the seller.

Historical Rate of New Introductions

In all businesses, as well as the art print business, new products are very important. I wanted to see how much revenue was being produced by Aaron Ashley's newer introductions versus old-time best sellers. Had Phil let the business rest on its laurels?

Many businesses are sold because the owner has become uninterested or is otherwise having problems. Often, toward the end, the seller takes his or her foot off the gas, not only in asset replenishment, but new product development as well. This is foolish, of course, since businesses do not always sell on time, and the seller may end up owning a shrinking business caused by their own shortsightedness. Still, as a buyer, you must be on the lookout for this. New products or services often are costly and have a long gestation period—so it's a good place to look for a decrease in activity that will hurt results after the purchase.

Validate Financial Statements

I trusted Phil, but this was a 9-million-dollar deal. Way too much for blind trust. I wanted to verify key elements on the financials with a bottom-up review of my own.

By bottom up I mean re-adding up each line on each invoice to see if it seems to total the top-line number in the general ledger. I frequently validate numbers by looking at them both in the aggregate (top down) and from the details (transactions) added up (bottom up).

Modeling the Future

I could argue in some sense that you should build the most comprehensive model of the future right at the start. But it never works that way. At first, it's not worth the time, since the likelihood of even making an offer is low. But as the parties grow closer, more time should be invested, and what's more, you know more about the business, so the model has a better chance of being close to reality. It really does need to be incremental.

Even so, the first model I build for an acquisition will save me loads of time down the road if I build it in a thoughtful manner. I set about building my main spreadsheet, making sure all the variables like sales, moving costs, investment in new product releases were in one handy spot, ripe for changing. I also assumed that we would pay Phil over time, so I built this into the spreadsheet as well. The first draft of the model was built even before I got the data feed, and after I had analyzed the data, the model went through several iterations.

The purpose of the model is to see if the future looks bright with all the expected changes, and likewise, to see how much the profit, ROI and cash flow change as things go wrong—which they of course will!

For the main variables, I adjusted them up and down and looked at the effect, to see just how sensitive they were. Not surprisingly, the biggest, most sensitive variables were:

1.   Our own sales level (not counting the acquisition).
2.   Aaron Ashley's post-acquisition sales.
3.   The purchase price (all its possible components).
4.   The timing of payouts of the purchase price.
5.   The amount of investment in inventory over time, both for replenishment of older items and new items.

Given that Aaron Ashley's sales had dropped in the past year, and given that I knew without doubt that their past 24 months of new product releases were doing horribly, it was clear there was a high likelihood the sales downtrend would continue.

With all the analysis and modeling, the next step is to make a decision. If you're independently wealthy, you just make the decision. But many of us have to turn to boards, partners, or investors to get the green light.

Key Concerns

After some spirited discussion at the board level, some key concerns emerged.

- Why buy a company where the new products have such a poor ROI?

This was a question that I had been asking myself as well. The answer was in understanding the performance dynamics of the different product lines. Since Aaron Ashley published traditional art, not tied to decorating trends, its products tended to sell steadily for many years. Occasionally it would get lucky and fall into a trend, but that was not the company's strategy. Our business, on the other hand, worked hard to identify the trends and publish hot images. But these images had a very short life span on average, and after three years or so sales would drop off quickly. Although I didn't have enough data to compute it, I argued that the net present value (NPV) of an Ashley piece did rival that of our average piece, even if the payback period for the initial investment was much longer.

Business is really about return on investment (ROI). If I must choose between internal expansion and an acquisition, I must compare the ROI of each. If I can do better expanding internally, why acquire? All of the opportunities for growth must be compared to see which has the best returns.

This, of course, only considers the traceable financial gains from each alternative. Integrating an acquisition eats up an enormous amount of time and corporate focus, but on the other hand, new ideas, practices and relationships are inherited that often benefit the buyer in unexpected ways. The costs and benefits in this are very hard to measure.

Likewise, starting new businesses and projects internally is also really wasteful as your internal team will make the same mistakes that every other entrant made when they started. But of course, you don't have to pay the seller anything....

I did concede that because of the slow payback and steady sales over time, it was not necessary to pour large investments of new imagery into Aaron Ashley, but instead to publish a steady trickle of timeless, traditional art. I also suggested that we should work hard to find any decorative trends within the traditional look and publish those into Ashley. They would be faster sellers at the start, then drift down to the slower, steady selling state as the trends passed.

It's the nature of most traditions—they're never completely out of style for everyone. Some percentage of the population always likes and buys traditional goods.

I further argued that our company, post acquisition, would have much greater breadth of product lines, covering the market from contemporary to traditional, and this latest large acquisition would place us in the league of the biggest companies in the industry. It would mean that more of our customers would turn to us as a first-choice supplier and would look to others only if we didn't have what they needed.

- Would this acquisition reduce our cash flow? If this acquisition drained cash from the existing business, one side effect would be that we would not be able to publish as much art of our own, which typically had a better ROI. How could I justify this?

I wanted to make sure that everyone understood that this acquisition would help our bottom line immediately, as it would be making a big contribution toward our overhead, even at the start, and after a year or two when we planned to consolidate warehousing and shipping, it would contribute even more. On top of that, their bottom line was better than ours. Not only was the bottom line better, but the contribution margin was better as well.

Cash flow impacts were much more uncertain. Assuming that we borrowed the down payment, and that sales of Ashley products were not less than 20% under forecast, we would have enough after-tax free cash flow from the Aaron Ashley products to pay the seller note, service the bank debt, and print a little new product. If Aaron Ashley sales dropped more than 20% below target, it would need to be the first brand to lose its budget for new products, since it needed less new product anyway to sustain itself, and because the payback period on such new product was the slowest.

Of course, all of this assumed a price a bit below the seller's target and a four-year payment plan. If sales were on target, the free cash flow would allow us to pay off the bank in about a year.

In the real world, either scenario was quite good actually. Most of the time, the buyer has to put in equity that stays in for a long time, while getting (hopefully) annual returns that compensate for the use of the equity in the business. We were looking to put no new equity into the business and pay for it out of cash flow generated by the business. That's an aggressive stance.

Our ownership at the time was not interested in putting more equity into the business, so if I was to do the deal, I had to do it with modest borrowing and the bulk of it with free cash flow. This is not ideal. I love growing and building businesses and am comfortable with the risks that go with it. In an ideal world, the CEO should find investors (or partners) that share his or her objectives.

- We would have to borrow from the bank for the down payment, whatever it would be. Would we be able to do so? If so, what flexibility would this leave us? With personal guarantees by all owners in place, was this deal important enough to risk my (and all owners') personal net worth?

I had plenty of experience to know what most banks can and will do. When I worked the numbers, we had the financials to justify a nice step-up in borrowing. Several of the ratios, however, started to approach cautionary limits. This meant that there would not be much room to go back to the bank for more if we needed it.

The old maxim that banks don't lend you money when you need it most is kind of true. If we had borrowed for this deal and then missed our sales or profitability targets, we would need more. But a bank, seeing that we were not fully in control of our business and were having trouble forecasting, would be quite nervous about getting further into bed with us. Add to that the fact that if we missed our targets in sales and profits, the very numbers they look at (certain key financial ratios) may well be in the danger zone, another reason not to extend further credit to us. It is not the bank's role in commerce to get companies out of real trouble. They're more about providing liquidity to help you grow.

When we had established this banking relationship some years ago, we had chosen a smaller local bank so we could be closer to the real decision makers. But about two years prior, the small local bank was bought by a regional bank. Then, about a month prior to my board meeting, a very large bank had purchased the regional bank. So far, the old crew was still in place and was saying that everything would be the same. *Of course they would say that.* But a small worry flag had gone up in my mind. I chose not to mention that to the board.

- What happens if sales fall off—either our own sales or Aaron Ashley's? At what point do we run into trouble?

It was no fun thinking about this. If we did this deal, we would be on the hook for more borrowings from the bank and at least some portion of fixed payments to Phil. Phil had stated that he wanted them all to be fixed payments, but I hadn't given in on this point yet.

If Aaron Ashley's sales went much below 20% off of projections, and if our company's sales were much more than 5% off historical levels, we would have to make strong cutbacks in new product releases and staffing. Of course, if we could buy Aaron Ashley for less, then we'd have more room in a downturn. It didn't help any that our most recent quarter had ended down. The first week of October, sales had been sluggish, although they often are at the start of the month. You can't project a month based on the first week of sales, but it still affects your nerves and confidence, especially when staring at big new fixed financial commitments.

- How could the seller be encouraged to make this work well for us?

With the structure Phil had indicated he wanted, there was no incentive for Phil to help us. He wanted a fully fixed payout, without conditions. I assured the board that he was a "good guy" and had an emotional investment in seeing the company succeed. But that's a pretty weak position.

Yes! *Doing an acquisition is a lot of work.* This chapter has been about the analysis part—the studying of the details so that all the important facts and risks are exposed to your scrutiny. I strongly encourage that you take plenty of time to dig into the analysis to see what you find without too much pressure to race to the end and make a decision about buying the business or what you should pay for it.

As you discover things, note them and you'll start to complete the tapestry that is a business. The impact of some will become obvious immediately, but many will take time to see how they affect the business and what your stance should be about them.

Data Mining Blow by Blow
(This section is an expansion of ideas from page 67.)

One of my primary tools in acquisitions is my ability to take huge piles of data and in short order slice and dice them to get to underlying truths about a business. In this chapter I show you what I generally do, in detail.

Clean Up the Data

Data being imported from other systems is almost always dirty. Not dirty in the illegal sense, but dirty in that often through the importing process, odd problems are created that cause constant stumbling down the road. As an example, the most common and noxious is having the space character (as in what you'll get when you hit the space bar on your keyboard) attached to data. So if you search for the word "cat" and in the data is "[space]cat," (in other words a space in front of the word) you won't get a result. *Of course, what makes it so noxious is the [space] is actually an invisible character,* so it's hard to notice. Also leading spaces mess up sorting too. Access has a function called "Trim" that fairly quickly removes all the leading and trailing spaces.

Other common problems are columns of numbers that import as text fields, not numeric fields. Date fields can import incorrectly for a variety of reasons. Sometimes there are boatloads of empty records that can be deleted.

Relationships between the tables must be understood and created. Lost children (records that should relate to

176

another table but seem to have no matching entry) have to be spotted, assessed, and cleaned up. I could go on and on, but I won't. It all takes only a few hours to do a good thorough job of this. Most of the time it can be completed alone—although sometimes one finds the data so broken or odd that a conversation is needed with the data source, and occasionally another table of data is required.

Wade around in the Data

The next step is to wade around in the data a bit. Seeing all the entries in the tables helps understand what is there. For example, I needed to call Aaron Ashley to decode a field called "customer type," which was populated with either a 1, 2, 4 or 5. I was informed what the numbers meant.

I wish it were as simple as getting the answers to known questions. It is not. While there are some known questions (e.g. "What are the best sellers?"), much of the value from "wading around in the data" comes from a curious mind.

What does that mean? It means as you look at the data in different ways, you notice things that are clues to understanding what is going on. (This is true not only about acquisitions but all data mining.) The moment you see those clues, you adjust your inquiry to focus in on them and disprove or confirm your hypothesis.

This is high-level work. Most administrative assistants and even many at the managerial level are linear in their thinking and wish to complete an assigned task. That doesn't cut it. Not only do you need (or need to be) a

177

non-linear, curious thinker, but a strong foundation in math helps too—to calculate new fields that highlight patterns—percentages, ratios, cumulative totals, and more.

Here is what I did.

I sorted each table (ascending, then descending) on many fields, looking for oddities. For example, one HUGE transaction (debit or credit) can bias the overall picture. This could be an attempt to pump up numbers, a data entry mistake, or a valid entry. I looked for small ones too. Anything odd or possibly significant goes on what I call my "List of 1000 questions," to which I seek answers.

I created useful new fields (columns). For example, I often want to look at progressions over time. I parse (break up) the date field into two new fields called "Month" and "Year." So if an invoice was created on February 17, 2000, I populate the field called "Month" with "2" and the field called "Year" with "2000." This is all done quickly with the "Year" and "Month" functions in Access.

With these handy columns in place, I added up the sales from each item sold on each invoice to match the financial statements. Good news: The numbers roughly matched what was reported by Ashley. I also added up the cost of goods sold associated with each sale to see if that matched too. I never found any significant irregularities in the Aaron Ashley books, or in fact any of the four companies' books that I acquired. Any irregularities I did find were normal irregularities—e.g., an especially great month was created not by sales of product but by the release of a new catalog (which is sold in this industry).

I use the invoice data to look at rate of sales of all items. Sometimes you can get inventory history files that have aggregated historical data already in them. This is extra nice but not always available. Also, history files like this can drift way off if the computer system they were built on was unstable. As I discovered the top sellers, I found them in the printed catalog to look at them and categorized them for later analysis. I also count (using a function, not by hand) the number of times an item is ordered, so I can tell if the velocity of the item stems from a lucky big order, or from broad-based demand.

I then compare the rate of sales in a given period of time to the inventory level of that item and create a column called "Days of Supply" so I can sort by it and zoom in to overstocks (that inventory has little value) and understocks or stockouts, where new investment may be required to replenish inventory.

Be careful about sellers letting important inventory run low or dry in an attempt to shift the cost of replenishment to the seller. In most cases, the deal documents will require the seller to run the business in the "ordinary course of business"—which means they should run it as through they are not about to sell the business. Of course, this leaves a lot of room for interpretation, and the buyer clearly needs to be the "policeman" to find breaches of this rule and demand a lower price, or sale price adjustments. Another common "trick" is to hold a "sale" in the last days of owning the business, trying to pull orders forward in time so the seller gets the money

Key customers come to life easily with this level of analysis. I transferred the top customers to Excel, and then flagged those that we already knew (most of them), but there were a number we didn't. Quickly, I had displayed percentages based on revenue generation.

Suppliers in this industry are important too—and are called artists. I pulled out sales by artist.

As I spent more and more time tying data to actual pictures of the art prints, I started wondering how well their new attempt at more contemporary art was doing. I made a list of all the pieces I considered contemporary (about 40 of them) and extracted the sales on those items. From the same "batch" of new product releases, I also extracted the imagery that was more traditional and gave it the same treatment. I also, using our production costs as a basis (different size prints have different unit costs), identified a form of return on investment, so I could compare different sizes of prints and different size groupings of prints on a fair basis.

When I say, "I made a list," it is always digital—in Excel, or in an Access table. Once the list is made, I link it to my database so I can create queries to get my answers. I do use a pen in the process—usually to jot down odd items so I don't forget the specifics. When I'm done I generally have a few pages of really messy scribbled notes, which I discard.

I ended up with the following tables in my report:

Chart 1: Inventory and Sales Analysis

I listed the top 80 sellers, with the following columns:
1. Item (stock number)
2. Catalog Page Number (so we could look at the image)
3. Qty Sold
4. # of Orders (how many orders carried this item, in the period analyzed)
5. Total Sales (revenue generated)
6. Description
7. Artist Name
8. Size of Print (inches)
9. Average Price after Discount
10. List Price
11. Average Discount. I can't get excited about high-discount closeout sales. This identifies them. Also, pricing and discounting is one of two major components of gross margin, and customers expect to get the same discounts after acquisition as before (or they get mad and go away).
12. $ Percentile. (What percent of total sales does this one item contribute?) Concentration of any kind must be investigated to see if it will likely continue, or go away. Either way, it still represents risk.
13. Stock Percentile. (What percent of the total inventory does this one item constitute?)
14. Inventory On Hand.
15. Cumulative Sales Revenue. Since this was a top performer list, this cumulative column showed

aggregate concentration—for example in the case of Aaron Ashley, these top 80 items constituted 50% of total sales.

16. Cumulative Stock. The same for stock items; helped to see how much of the storage warehouse was really producing the revenues.

Chart 2: Inventory Sales on Stock Analysis by Percentile of Sales Dollars

The concentration of sales in key items was dramatic. So I created a summary of the whole chart above, mostly by deciles. It was just 15 lines, but it showed the huge bulk of slow sellers, accounting for little of the sales but taking up most of the warehouse.

Chart 3: 1999-2000 Customer Sales, Descending

1. Customer Number. I listed the top 75 customers.
2. Customer Name
3. 1999 Sales
4. Projected 2000 Sales
5. Change Year-over-Year. Customer relationships are an asset, just like inventory. Of course, they don't appear on the balance sheet (but they should). Growing sales in the aggregate is good, but zooming in to see the details is critical. For example, are new customers offsetting consistent declines in existing customers? If so, why? This level of analysis should be done in every business, not just when acquiring.
6. State
7. Our Customer Now? (Yes/No and comments)

Chart 4: 1999 Sales by Artist

1999 Sales by Artist						
Units Sold	# of Orders	Sales	Cumulative Sales	Artist	% of Total Sales	Cum. Percent
39337	3672	$415,339	$415,339	JUDY	12.3%	12.3%
21595	2035	$367,958	$583,297	MONET	9.6%	21.9%
Precise numbers have been changed to protect confidentiality.						

I laid out which artists' images were producing the most revenue. I listed only the top 40, which accounted for 75% of all sales. My columns were:

1. Units Sold
2. The number of orders that carried that artist's prints
3. Revenues Generated
4. Cumulative Revenues (from the top seller down)
5. The Name of the Artist
6. The Percentage of Total Revenues
7. The Cumulative Percentage of Total Sales

As I worked on this, I noticed that half of the top artists' sales came from one customer. I noted it as a risk element.

Chart 5: 1999 Sales by Item by Customer
Listed in Descending Order

Again, I was looking for concentration. This report—just the top page—was quite interesting. For example, the Spanish distributor Phil took to dinner with us spent the most money on catalogs—more than he'd spent on any individual product.

A full forty percent of Aaron Ashley's second-to-largest customer's volume came from one item. I took a peek at the item and was really quite surprised. Surprised means concerned, since I clearly didn't understand it. Not understanding is bad, because if I am to run the acquired business successfully, I really need to understand all things that contribute to its success.

Chart 6: Success of New Product

In this business, like most, new product launches are costly and risky. But we do them because they are necessary to keep the attention of our customers. Once we can see how an item is selling, we order appropriate quantities, so the risk becomes much lower. I decided to zoom in on Aaron Ashley's new releases and measure them, and I did the same thing for our new releases, so I'd have a comparison.

I wrote, "AA published Supplement 1 in January of 1999, covering all releases since the 1997 catalog debut. They have steadily published since then, and plan to release a new supplement in November of 2000. In each release, some prints were what one would expect from AA—

traditional museum reproductions, or images from their top artist, Penney. Other images were trend based, primarily upon the advice of a new member of the Aaron Ashley team. Below are the results, which are poor."

	Supplement 1	
	1999 Sales Data	
	Core AA Items	Trend Items
# of items		
Qty of Prints Sold		
Avg per item/mo		
Ttl Revenue		
Avg Price		
Above 50/mo		
Above 30/mo		
	2000 Sales Data	
	Core AA Items	Trend Items
# of SKUs		
Qty of Prints Sold		
Avg per SKU/mo		
Ttl Revenue		
Avg Price		
Above 50/mo		
Above 30/mo		

The specific data is blank for confidentiality reasons.

The results weren't just poor. They were *very* poor! Essentially, Aaron Ashley's core new product was selling less than 1/3 of what our new products sold at the same point in their lifestyle. Their trend products were just abysmal, complete failures.

Their trend program would have to be immediately dumped and no new investment would go into it. For the core program, it was either broken as well, or the traditional, off-trend art had a very different selling pattern—perhaps they were slow sellers, but with high longevity. Beware of applying your assumptions and your way of doing business to the seller's business. In every industry, competitors have their tricks. Keep your mind open and be slow to condemn what you observe as "bad." Dig for value—and listen to the seller's reasons for doing what they do.

A few items were timeless images that some percentage of the population will always like. They never made our top seller charts, but 100 of them, selling steadily over time, made a big collective contribution to our sales.

So I set off to validate that thought. I asked for estimated dates of first publication (their computer didn't save this tidbit automatically), looked at average discounts (steady sellers usually sell at higher prices, but in smaller quantities), and other gems the data could reveal. I already knew that the new product wasn't accounting for much of the total revenue.

With projected cash flow in mind, I started to doubt whether this steady-selling traditional line would need the heavy, regular investment in new product. This would significantly brighten the cash flow outlook if it were true.

Since I had less than 2 years' detailed data, I took the 5 years' financial statements I had requested and spread them. "Spreading financials" means putting each year's data in one column, right next door to the next year's data. Usually percentages are added as well, often both year-to-year change columns, and common size percentage columns (like percentage of sales/assets columns).

1999 was their best year in the past 4. So much for the ill effect of bad new product releases. But 2000 was looking down by about 12%. Phil attributed it to his inattention to the business due to his eyesight problems. Maybe that was true. Maybe it wasn't.

Gross Margin was nice and steady over the years, and so was profit before taxes, except in the current year when it dropped about 20% due to the decline in volume. Still, the bottom line was nice.

Forecast Details

This section is continued from the comment on page 87).

Just as a book is broken up into chapters and then paragraphs, so too should be a financial model. The math should reflect the way an analyst (or a CEO) thinks through the problem. It's easier to understand and validate the results that way.

I created two main sections for the model.

1. The main business (including the two acquisitions we had already made).
2. Aaron Ashley adjusted as though we owned it.

For the main business (the acquirer), I had the following rows, with a 5-year forecast:

1. Sales. I had a constant where I could adjust year-over-year growth. One click and the model would shift from decline to growth.
2. Net profits. Based on a percentage of sales, also tied to a single cell where I could adjust the number easily. Note: Profit is not cash. But if your balance sheet accounts (assets and liabilities) stay constant, profit (after taxes) will become cash. I put profit in here because it was not going to stay constant (it needed to go up), and then in a "cash" section of the model I could add and subtract balance sheet items.
3. Payments to sellers. These were on their own line, as they were quite lumpy. Some of them were after tax payments, and affected only the balance

sheet. My goal for the forecast was to see the effect on our cash flow, so it took more than just the income statement to get the right number at the bottom.

4. Inventory adjustments. Any change in balance sheet accounts either uses or supplies cash to the business. Inventory was our biggest asset. We regularly wrote off inventory (and actually threw it away), and regularly bought more inventory. Decisions about how much inventory to discard were driven by profit planning, tax planning, by space in the warehouse, and of course, by having enough obsolete stock (that we were willing to discard) in the warehouse. Write-offs would help us reduce our tax burden in the main company, which in turn would help the cash flow. Estimates of this were input into this line.

5. Taxes. The bane of profit is taxes, and they must be paid in cash. We took these out of projected cash flows.

6. Capital expenditures. We took estimates of this and pulled them out of cash flow.

7. Other balance sheet items. We estimated the sum of other balance sheet changes (A/R, non-bank debt of all types, etc.) and plugged the numbers in. I usually leave new borrowings to the last, as my plug figure. So if I end up in the hole, I know I must borrow that amount to pay the bills.

8. Cash available after tax, existing business. This is the amount that theoretically could be used to buy Aaron Ashley.

Understanding a large acquisition (relative to the existing business) must take into account risks in both businesses. So the second part of the spreadsheet focused on Aaron Ashley.

My rows:

1. Sales
2. Contribution Margin. The contribution margin is sales minus variable costs. Since we were buying a business just like ours, we wouldn't need to duplicate the overhead, so I discarded it. Of course, having a bigger business automatically means more overhead (trust me), so one must be careful with this logic. Of course variable costs never go away—in this case, cost of goods sold and royalties are the largest. Another category of costs is fixed direct overhead, which normally wouldn't be deducted from sales to get the contribution margin number. But for the first 2 years we planned to keep the NY warehouse running, so all those costs would not change. For simplicity's sake, I reduced the contribution margin in the first 2 years by those expenses, rather than make an additional line in the model.
3. Price Increase Revenues. We had looked at Aaron Ashley prices and found them to be below market. Phil agreed that a price increase made sense. So we planned on a 17% price increase, then deducted about half of it, assuming some level of price elasticity. Simply put, when you raise prices, some number of people will no longer buy the product. In business school they call it the

"price elasticity of demand," and they talk about it as though it was measurable. In reality, in small to medium size businesses it is nearly impossible to quantify, even after the fact. Although you may change prices at a certain point in time, there are so many other factors—the economy, your new products, competition, sales and marketing efforts and more—that it's hard to tie down the effect of a price increase. No customers will call you to tell you that they were *happy* with the price increase—only the angry people will call. All this is to say that we made our best guess in the model.

4. Inventory Write-Offs. The Ashley deal was inventory heavy, and we suspected that after a year of ownership we would be able to identify inventory that should be written off. This would reduce profitability and taxes, helping cash flow.

5. Amortization of Intangibles. This is a tax write off we could get as a buyer.

6. Income Tax Expense. (This was just from Ashley's earnings.)

7. Cash Contribution from Operations. Not the real bottom line, unfortunately. There was another big outflow, namely.....

8. Principal Payments to Seller.

9. Interest Payments to Seller. I did this on a separate line so I could use the principal balance times an interest rate to make the interest expenses automatically adjust as we played with principal payments.

10. Tax Savings on Interest. (The more interest I pay, the less taxes I must pay).

11. Total Cash Outflow to Seller. (This was so I could tell Phil how rich he'd be.)
12. Net Cash Flow Usage. (Contribution from Ashley)

The very last line was the combined cash usage or contribution we'd have to work with if the deal went through.

Chapter 15: Essays on Business

Five Reasons to Extend Your Hand

(Continued from the chapter endnote on page 6.)

Summary: This essay explains why having even a shallow relationship with competitors can be very productive. It debunks some of the biggest fears about such relationships and suggests some tools to help with the process.

"Hello, I'm Robert Sher with Bentley, and I just wanted to introduce myself and meet you."

I first heard this form of greeting on a sales training tape some 20+ years ago. The notion is that most people find it very hard to reject a person directly. If you offer a reason or purpose for your visit, it is much easier to reject your reason than to reject you as a human being.

Still, despite all this, it is really hard for most people, myself included, to reach out and make new friends without an immediate need.   Double or triple that difficulty if the other party is a competitor.   So we procrastinate and hesitate.

Overcoming that hesitancy will set you apart and will create great opportunities, especially if you contemplate ever buying competitors' businesses, or selling your own. It's really up to you, since most of the competitors' CEOs will never overcome this barrier themselves. My argument goes as follows:

Drop your preconceived notions about the mindset of your competitors. Many assume that competitors automatically dislike each other and would do anything to defeat each other. Certainly all competition is fighting for the order, and no one has any remorse when they take that order from you. But among small-to-medium-sized businesses, the competition is all in the same boat and shares the same hopes and dreams as you do. As a result of the shared experience, they take some comfort in knowing that they are not alone, and they like to share, in some small part, the experience with a peer like you. Most are just trying to make a living and grow modestly—not to become a monopoly and dominate the world. You are probably not their biggest obstacle or even close.

Meeting competitors is not about becoming best friends. The primary goal is to break the ice that naturally exists between two people who have no relationship. Some idle chatter, followed up by light periodic communication does 90% of the work. Being realistic about what you are shooting for makes it much easier to take those first steps. Sometimes you will be able to move forward to a "trading information" stage, where you may tell bits of information of use to them in exchange for information of use to you.

Ease up on your paranoia. Too many CEOs worry that passing out any information will give the competition a huge edge that will come back to bite them. I strongly disagree. While there certainly are a handful of upcoming strategic moves that should be kept completely confidential, most information about your business is not actionable by a competitor. So what if they find out your top line is 8 million instead of 4 million? Is there something different they will suddenly do with that piece of knowledge? Will they try to grow more fervently than before? I doubt it. Will they try to copy you? I'll bet they've been doing that already. Turn the tables, and pretend you got some basic information about your competition. Does it change much of what you are doing? Probably not. I'm not saying to disclose willy-nilly. Give information only when you must, and give it carefully. But don't be so apprehensive that you don't extend your hand to your competition.

They might be interesting people. Meeting and getting to know interesting people can be fun. Why not enjoy yourself while doing business? This is the best mindset that you can have, as people will sense your curiosity and interest in them, and most people love this. Believe me, some people live the most interesting lives, often quite different from our own. When reaching out to business owners, CEOs and executives, chances are slim that they will be "boring" if you stick around long enough to let them show their true colors. Showing interest in their personal lives (as opposed to their business) is encouraged. I do admit that some will be boring to you, and if they are just spend less time with them. You don't have time for hundreds of friends anyway, nor are you likely to buy that many businesses!

Key Takeaways

1. Take the initiative to extend your hand, just for the sake of "getting to know one another." Keep in contact occasionally.

2. Don't assume most competitors won't want to talk with you. Most of your competitors don't hate you.

3. Don't be afraid to trade non-strategic business information. Having a small give-and-take in a relationship builds trust and comfort. Of course, don't tell them everything, and make what you learn from them count!

4. Getting to know other business leaders in your industry can be personally rewarding and enjoyable. If they like you, you are much more likely to be selected as the preferred buyer of their business when they are ready.

Give First, Then Ask

(Continued from the comment on page 6.)

Summary: Start relationships with others by giving them something of value first. Quality people will give back, creating a cycle of generosity.

In the book, I spotted a key buyer and informed the competitor I was just getting to know about the big opportunity soon to pass by his booth.

Too many people focus on their own personal gain when they think about how to connect with another person. Admittedly, we are all motivated by the hope of personal gain, but the direct approach is worn out. Make guilt your friend, and take a two-step approach. *Give first, then ask for what you want.* It seems simple, and it is. Before you make the call, or make the approach, try and think up something that would help the other party. It could be information, or maybe it's a pizza during the setup of their show booth. Then just give it away. Don't ask for the return favor in the next breath. Just give it to them, and let the equity in the relationship shift to you. Most people are loath to "owe you," and will work to give you something back, in some form or another.

For a number of years I had a business partner who did this unfailingly. He'd keep hard candies in his pocket and would drop a few on your desk all the time. He'd always grab the tab at lunch. He'd loan people money in hard times. He loved to entertain. He'd buy people little treats. *He was generous.* I often wondered how he ever

197

kept any money in his bank account, and at first I thought he was nuts. But over time, I saw how many people felt a special bond with him and how his generosity served him well. Honestly, it was not just his "giving" that did the trick (he had other positive traits) but it was a key part of his success.

Ideally, if you give regularly in a relationship, and the other person is giving back regularly, you will both forget who is next to reciprocate and wind up with some level of commitment to each other, perfect for setting the stage for business deals. But if the other person turns out to be a taker, never returning anything of value, then you will have learned a valuable lesson about their character, and should be cautious (in fact reticent) about doing any deal with them.

The Benefits of Leading in Industry Organizations

(Continued from the comment on page 12.)

Summary: Getting involved in industry organizations as a volunteer/leader pays big dividends for only a small amount of time and energy. Read about specific benefits as well as a few words of caution.

There is a strange truth that only a few seem to really know and embrace. By giving you can gain in so many ways. I do believe this is generally true in the universe. But I want to focus on an industry trade show a few years back, where I was in no less than four gatherings with our industry leaders. These people were leaders because they took time away from their own businesses—large and small—to contribute to their community, in this case the art and framing industry.

It was a few years ago when John, my competitor (and now my friend as well), invited me and many others to a meeting to talk about our industry and the formation of an association. From that start, he led me into the world of giving back to our industry, and I cannot thank him enough.

And as I go to meetings, I see others get involved and watch them reap the benefits. All of the industry organizations are hungry for active participation. The underlying benefit is networking with powerful people and companies in your industry who will begin to know who you are, will respect your contribution and capabilities, and will want to work with you on some level when an opportunity presents itself.

But it takes some faith. At first, it's not clear how it could increase sales or profits. And the urgency of day-to-day business will seem more important. But if you contribute consistently, and with the same discipline and acumen you apply to your own business or job (albeit with fewer hours per week), the benefits will come back to you.

All it takes is:
- Showing up at meetings. Sometimes they are boring, but you're being seen and heard by other leaders of the industry.
- Speaking at the meetings, even if just once or twice. People really notice you when you speak, and they appreciate any contribution.
- Spending as little as an hour every two weeks—helping in some way. Writing, calling someone, getting on a committee.

Ask yourself what person, what group, or what committee has some potential of helping you? Who would it be wise to get to know? After all, who you know can mean everything in life, and what better way to get to know the people who can open doors for you—than by working shoulder-to-shoulder with them to help others? Now this is starting to sound selfish, but the reality is that we live in a busy world, and almost no one is so successful that they have the luxury of time. Yet if we can help our industry at the very same time as we help our own company or our own career, we can afford to donate more time to the cause.

Some of the personal benefits I've observed for myself and others are:

- The self-gratification of helping others—it just feels good.
- The accolades and respect of peers and leaders in the industry.
- Confidence building for staff and new managers.
- Leadership skill building.
- The inside scoop on opportunities for participants' businesses.
- Public relations for the participants.
- Job opportunities.
- New customers.
- New business partners.
- Opportunities to buy and sell businesses.
- Making new friends.

Of course, getting involved with your hand out never works—it always takes time—as in months or years, and the genuine desire to contribute is a pre-requisite. And while helping charities in your own hometown or any other non-industry-related cause also does return great benefits, your industry is the closest community to your livelihood—so the translation to dollars is generally faster. I do hope that the more material success you have encourages you to contribute still more—in a never-ending cycle of giving and receiving.

This is especially true of leaders who have already "done their time." We all deserve a rest from service, yet new people are always coming into the industry, and new opportunities will arise—and those new people with new opportunities may not even know who the old leaders are. If they do, they may be afraid to make the approach. Why give the benefits of personal involvement away to the next generation of entrants into our industry?

Now I *should* make the point that you *should* help your industry because it's the right thing to do. If that alone makes you get involved, my hat's off to you. But if not, think about this strange truth in this strange world—the more you give away, the more you'll receive. Then pick up the phone and get involved.

The above article first appeared in Décor Magazine.

Key Takeaways

1. Get involved in your industry organizations.
2. Put in a little time on a regular basis, working your way toward some level of leadership.
3. Nurture the relationships you start to build, and make sure your character and competencies shine through.

Get Out!

(Continued from the comment on page 16.)

Summary: Getting your body out of your office and face to face with the marketplace and its players is critical. Valuable insights will be gleaned.

I just got off the phone with a good customer who two years ago placed his first order and is now growing steadily. After thanking him for his business, which he expects to double next year, we began chatting. It turned out that he had been in our industry for over 15 years and had owned four galleries, selling limited editions and serigraphs. Since my company didn't sell limited editions, he hadn't been a customer. But about two years ago he discovered the world of truck jobbing, where he would manufacture wall decor, load up his truck, and make the rounds to furniture stores in his part of the country, selling his pictures at wholesale. He lamented, "I had no idea that such a business model even existed. Had I known this, I would have sold my galleries years earlier."

Every industry is rich with opportunity and diversity. There are many different types of businesses in each industry, of many sizes, most of which are successful. But you'll never know if you could be much happier (or much richer) using a different business model—if you don't get out, look around and learn.

- Get out of your office or shop, go visit retailers or distributors and ask where they get their products from, and if there is need or room for another supplier.

- Get out of your office or shop and visit your customers and ask them about their needs and how you could garner more of their business if you did things differently.
- Get out of your office and visit your suppliers, and ask them who their best customers are and what their business models are.
- Get out of your office and join an industry organization so you can make friends in the industry and pick their brains for ideas.
- Get out of your office and spend time on the internet to see what others in the industry are doing.
- Get out of your office and read the trade magazines that your customers (or prospective customers) are reading.
- Get out of your office and find a business to buy.
- Get out of your office and be curious, ask lots of questions, and keep an open mind.
- Get out of your office and educate yourself about your business environment. Even if no opportunity presents itself, you'll be better able to recognize one when it comes down the pike.

So there you have it. Get out!

The above article first appeared in Décor Magazine.

Key Takeaways

1. Get out of your office and into the marketplace.
2. Talk to people, and ask questions. Be curious.
3. Investigate with an open mind, looking for new ideas or new realities that will give you clues about shaping your business.

Inherently Wasteful

(Continued from comment on page 21.)

In the book, I lament that a trade show in Amsterdam netted no orders at all and hardly had any attendance. I put it in the "waste" column.

Summary: The process of trying new things in business will cause some inevitable waste of resources and time.   Don't let that discourage you, but the amount of waste can be managed.

Was it [the Amsterdam trade show] a waste? Surely. But was it avoidable waste? Maybe not.

For businesses to grow and expand, new things must be tried.   Our world is changing ever faster, and new products and services keep customers interested.   New processes and technology reduce costs or make possible new offerings. By definition, "new" means not tried and true. The greater the innovation or "jump" the greater the potential for both big gains as well as failures. It stands to reason that the process of trying new things will have plenty of mistakes along the way, and mistakes mean wasted efforts, wasted money and wasted resources. Waste is inherent in the process of innovation.

Of course, trying new things in business certainly can be either more or less wasteful.   The archetypical entrepreneur with a "Ready, Fire, Aim" mentality will have huge waste.   I am not advocating this. Commensurate with the scale of the risk, any new venture should be researched carefully. Take the time to rough out how much investment will be required (time and money) and what the likelihood of success is. In particular, prospective customers must be consulted.

Think phases. Sometimes, the most appropriate focus must be to understand how much must be spent to get to the next level of certainty. Efforts should be made to test on a smaller scale first (if applicable). Beware of trying more than one new thing, lest you spend a bunch of money and not know what worked (or didn't). So attending a new trade show in a new territory with new products is not a good endeavor to learn from. Clear expectations should be established, and limits to how deep in the hole the new venture should be allowed to go. Proper measures should be in place so everyone will be able to see the progress.

If you do it all right, you're still going to fail some of the time. It's easy to look back, with all the knowledge you gained through the attempt, and be critical of the decision. But that's not fair. If for any reason you feel so badly about failing at some new things, you'll be reticent to ever try anything new, which leads to stagnation and business decay. And yes, you *should* feel bad about business stagnation and decay.

A big side benefit of trying new things is that you'll discover something useful that was unexpected. When your intended initiative is failing, ask yourself: what does this mean and how can I find value for the company anyway? Attempting the new freshens our outlook on the business and the industry.

207

One last thing: Spend only what you can afford. Too many businesses have fallen in love with their own beliefs—so much so that they wind up in debt or unable to recover.

Key Takeaways

1. Keep trying new things regularly.
2. Do an appropriate amount of research and planning, and understand the level of risk you will be taking.
3. Expect that some will not succeed, and never use hindsight to "beat yourself up." Focus instead on learning.

Tending to the Important

(Continued from the comment on page 22.)

Summary: It's all too easy to lose focus from the really big important tasks in our lives and to busy ourselves with the seemingly urgent work. We pay for that in a big way in the end. Here are some tips about the way I fight this common battle.

In the story, I forgot to make a dinner date with Phil well in advance, and by the time I remembered he was all booked up. That meant I missed seeing him for a year, which isn't good for building a relationship.

It's really easy to get swept away by all the urgent things and details in our day-to-day work and forget about diligently, relentlessly pursuing the *important* things. Then we resentfully wonder how others around us with less skill and knowledge (in our opinion) seem to jump forward with big leaps of success. Why is this?

Usually it's because we all get deluged with urgent matters via phone, fax, e-mail, people walking in our office, even SMS now. These urgent details catch our attention, and because they are usually quick to be handled or resolved, and because they are making noise, we tackle them first. Then, as the end of the day comes we think, "Darn, I never even started working on such and such project that I was all fired up to do as I drove in this morning...." Another day slips by.

To fight this, we must first clarify in writing what is on our to-do list that is really important—the stuff of company building. Once clarified, we have to set goals and objectives with time-targets laid out. Post them and make it public, so that the important projects start to feel urgent too.

I've found that setting time aside to work on projects (I often work on them very early in the morning) is helpful, and that I sometimes do the work away from the distractions at the office.

If you can, deny yourself the good feelings we often get from accomplishing the urgent, but not important, tasks. At the end of a day when I've lost control of my time and ended not working on the important tasks, I am distinctly dissatisfied with myself, even if I made some excellent things happen.

Be sure to pay attention to your own behavior, and watch out for procrastination. Often choosing simple tasks over big intimidating projects is just procrastination at work. One cure for that is to break up the large projects into bite-size pieces and just tackle them one at a time—with each part having a deadline in writing.

Often making yourself accountable to others for the important projects helps. It could be your boss, your leadership team, or a fellow executive in a peer group. But knowing that someone will be asking you about your progress on a certain date spurs most of us into action.

One of the most important things in business is tending to your network. Who you know is a big deal, even if you can't tell right now how it will help. Set aside time to keep your network vibrant.

In the end, if you are **really** hungry for the outcome that you'll achieve if you do the important things, you'll push them to the top of the list and tackle them. Passion is your ally.

Key Takeaways

1. Clearly identify the important things on your "list" that will make a big difference for your future.
2. Set aside specific times of day that you will do only these things.
3. Feel GREAT when you accomplish the important things, but don't let yourself feel so good at the end of a day that you've mostly done the urgent work.

Good Reasons vs. Bad Reasons
(Continued from note on page 36)

Summary: One of the most important things to understand about sellers is why they want to sell. Don't expect that they'll just tell you. Surely they will tell you something, but it's not always the truth, or it's a half-truth. This essay identifies many of the common reasons sellers sell businesses.

Selling a business is a big change. Given that most people don't want to change, something typically is motivating the change. If the seller's business was about to hit the jackpot, trust me, he or she would not be selling.

Of course, there are legitimate reasons that a business owner would sell a business even in good times. For your sake, I hope that the business you buy will be on the block for what I call a "good" reason. That means it's good for the buyer.

Just as often, businesses are sold so that the owner can avoid an impending problem. He or she sees that the business will, in the future, perform more poorly, so better to sell it now. That's what I call a "bad" reason.

It's your job to discover all the reasons the seller is selling and to fully understand the impact they will have on your deal.

Without further ado, I'll run through the checklist. First we'll review the "good" reasons, then the "bad." When you start looking at a deal, come back to this essay and use it to insure that you are being thorough.

Good Reasons

1. Retirement. That's understandable. Not everyone wants to die with their boots on.
2. Burn-out/Boredom. It was fun for the seller for a number of years, but not so fun now. They want to move on. This is a good reason only if they have just begun to burn out. If they've been burnt out for a long time and have not been driving the business forward lately, look out.
3. Limits to Growth. The seller has a path to growth but can't get there himself. He lacks something. It's a good reason if you have what he lacks.
4. Needs Liquidity. This is a common limit to growth—the seller doesn't have enough money to allow the business to thrive.
5. Death. Pretty hard to fake this one, and most won't go this far just to get a better multiple on EBITDA!
6. Divorce. Divorce often requires liquidity—a legitimate reason to sell a large asset like a business.
7. Illness. Sadly, sometimes people get too sick to run the business. This played a key role in our acquisition of Aaron Ashley.
8. Estate or Family Reasons. Sometimes the family needs cash, and selling the business is what is required. Or estate taxes are due, and the only source of liquidity is the business.

9. Shareholder Disputes. Most partnerships run into trouble. Sometimes the best thing is to just sell the firm. It's true!

10. Sale of a Division That No Longer Fits In. This good reason relates more to conglomerates. Many times a great business is sold because it is too small or not a major area of focus for the main business.

11. Sale of a Subsidiary by a Foreign Owner. Another good reason, usually occurring in multi-nationals, or following an acquisition of a multi-business company.

12. Cash Needed for Another Part of the Business. Again, selling one division can generate needed cash for the main operation.

Bad Reasons

1. Competition Is Looming Large. The seller feels that in the next few years they will lose market share to strong competitors, and they wish to sell to a sucker who doesn't realize that.

2. Construction Imminent. Important only for retail, but road construction or shipping center remodeling can last for a long time and kill traffic. The seller seeks to shift the pain to you.

3. Obsolete Products or Knowledge. Change is everywhere, and if the seller realizes that their big advantage is about to be obscured by new technology or products on the horizon, they will wish to sell before doomsday arrives.

4. Lease Problems, Impending Increase. More of an issue for some than others; be sure to understand

what you will have to pay for your physical space. I've seen some old-line businesses in high-rent districts be profitable only because they had a very long-term lease at incredible rates. As soon as the lease goes up to market levels, they are gone. Avoid holding the bag when this happens.

5. Franchisor Problems. Much of the value of a franchise is based on the viability of the franchisor. Check this carefully so that you don't buy in near the end of a franchisor's life.

6. Aged Infrastructure about to Fail. Maybe the computer and phones work now, but how old are they, and how much life is left? Add to the caution, many-fold if the business has lots of essential equipment. Look for the bubblegum holding it all together.

7. A/R Problems. Never assume that A/R is collectible. It the seller really wants you to assume the collection risk, look out.

8. Supplier/Creditor Problems. In some businesses, supplier relationships are everything. If you had several exclusive dealerships for equipment and knew that you were going to lose them in the next year or two, wouldn't you try and sell quickly?

9. Changes in Marketplace or Technology. Some industries don't last forever. Is this one in trouble, or is it going through changes that will hurt the business?

10. Increased Cost of Debt. If the business is heavily leveraged, and rates are rising, be sure to factor this into your projections. Some businesses are really interest-rate sensitive.

11. Hostage to Others. Hey, Wal-Mart has just become their biggest customer. Time to sell, so that as they demand price reductions that devastate your margins (but to which you can't say no), you feel the pain and not the seller...

12. Buyer/Seller Strength Shift. The patent has three years left. Sell now, because without the patent, the seller won't have the control over the customers like they do now.

13. Internal Conflicts: Loss of Key Employees. The technical genius quit or died, or the charismatic rainmaker has left and the business is coasting.

14. Union Agreement Problems or an Impending Strike. Wouldn't that be a nasty surprise the month after closing on a deal!

15. Customer Concentration/Threat to Major Customer. Maybe the seller's business is fine, but the dominant customer is in trouble—best to sell before the house of cards collapses.

16. Impending Regulatory Headache: Tax Assessment/Audits, New Laws, Government Prosecutions, etc. Legislation can make or break a business. Make sure you know the tides in this area before buying in.

17. Outstanding Stock Options, Undisclosed Bonus Plans or Similar Arrangements. Dig into these kinds of details carefully. They can represent huge surprises and often are in place for your most valuable employees—so you can't choose not to pay them.

18. Industry/Business/Economy About to Begin a Down Cycle. Of course every seller would want to sell near the crest of a cycle. And you want to

buy just before the bottom of a downturn. Make sure you know where the cycle is before moving forward.

I'm sorry, you might now be feeling depressed. If so, re-read the "Good Reasons" section above!

Key Takeaways

1. Sellers don't want to tell you the true reason they are selling if they think it will hurt the price or likelihood of selling.
2. Be sure you fully understand the TRUE reasons why the seller is selling.
3. If they're selling to avoid upcoming problems, be certain that you DO know how to avoid those problems as the new owner, or that you've factored in the costs to the business.

Outside Board of Directors

(Continued from the note on page 77)

Summary: This essay speaks to the value of a "real" board of directors. It is not based on the events in this book's story, but examines an actual business that brought on outside directors and benefited greatly.

Most entrepreneurs had a boss in their earlier life. One of the big benefits of owning your own company is supposed to be freedom and independence from a boss. And it is, if you can avoid seeing the customers, the bank and the marketplace as your boss.

Ceil McCloy, CEO, and her husband Dave Dobson, Co-Founder, fled the corporate life and started their own business, Integrated Science Solutions, Inc. (ISSI). But by 2004, they had brought in two outside board members and ended up with only a 50% vote on the board. Is this a case of capitalistic recidivism, where these owners just can't take the freedom?

The Case

ISSI is one interesting business. Ever wonder how the government figures things out? Like what clothes future soldiers should wear to protect them but not weigh them down? Or what kind of wire is best for equipment in the nose cone of the shuttle? Or how to build a repository to contain nuclear waste safely for ten thousand years? ISSI bids on government contracts to answer science and engineering questions like these. When they win the contract, they assemble a team of top scientists who go to work.

Ceil was a corporate vice-president who quit her prior post: Dave had already left his prior job and was a technical consultant. After Ceil left her job, they decided that they could do it on their own just as well, if not better. Ceil's prior focus had been as operations manager with targeted business development experience, and Dave's focus had been primarily technical as a senior scientific contributor. As their first outside board member they selected Nick Trentacoste. Ceil had worked for many years with Nick at her prior employment, where he had been Director of Marketing and Business Development for 25 years. He understood the industry, had connections and relationships in all the right places, and had just started a consulting practice on his own. She brought him on as a board member as well as a consultant.

Formal board meetings are held twice a year, on schedule. Just like a CEO of a large company, she prepares for them ahead of time and presents the financials and progress on strategic decisions. Nick has voted both for and against Ceil. He has crafted compromises when Ceil and Dave held nearly opposite strategic opinions. ISSI flies Nick and his wife from Washington, D.C. to California twice a year and plans fun itineraries for Nick's wife. As a consultant, Nick makes introductions in pursuit of contracts, reviews bids (they are very complex), and provides strategic direction.

The cost: About \$5,000 in annual expenses, plus about \$15,000 a year paid in hourly consulting fees for Nick's business development activities. The benefits: Millions in contracts that would not have been landed otherwise, and an honest, experienced voice on the board.

In mid-2004, they carefully brought on Don, a second board member. A retired military officer, his knowledge and credentials are different from Nick's and are of strategic assistance in broadening the base of agencies that work with ISSI.

Today, the board looks well credentialed—a critical issue in ISSI's world. Top scientists want to hire on with top firms, led by people that command their respect, and they look at the Director roster. Likewise, agencies awarding contracts for large and critical projects look for credibility in the Directors of firms they work with.

The Analysis

Businesses of all sizes look to the outside for help, hiring consultants for all manner of needs. For better or for worse, corporations are legally required to have an oversight group—the Board of Directors. Too many businesses pay lip service to the notion of the Board's role, just barely fulfilling legal requirements. But bolstering the Board's role in oversight of your business can be very beneficial, as it has for ISSI.

Benefits

Having outside board members forces the CEO and the top team to set aside time to work on strategic, board-level issues and formally present them. The effort and time to develop the presentation forces disciplined thinking and planning, which is a hugely beneficial process. Immediately following is the review of the proposal by a Board that can evaluate it objectively and dispassionately and base a decision on a broader experience base than the CEO or other owners alone can have.

The existence of outside board members adds credibility. Lenders take comfort in the experience and oversight they provide. Employees, especially professional ones, can see that the CEO is held accountable. As a result, the professional atmosphere in which management resides is enhanced. Recruitment of senior people becomes easier. Likewise, in industries where credentials are important, the status and respect of board members transfers directly to the company.

Most board members take individual initiative too, and actively participate in building the business. Board members who are more highly paid are generally expected to bring in clients, make introductions, assist in financing matters and more. ISSI's technique of mixing low-paying board membership with hourly consulting fees is another way to achieve the same result.

221

Ownership Must be Ready

For some owners, it's more about control than success. If that's you, avoid outside directors. Having outside directors that you overrule or ignore is a waste for both parties. Alternatively, if you want your business to be all it can be, and you are ready to travel a variety of roads leading to that success, you are ready for outside directors.

The CEO and all owners of the firm must realize that having outside directors is a time commitment. Time to prepare for meetings, time to keep them informed about developments in the firm, and time to socialize with them when they are in town. Like a real company, directors have power, and respect must be shown for the role they play. Similarly, outside directors cost money too—less if they are local, less if they are eager to serve, but still, it takes money changing hands to create a sense of mutual obligation.

The Right Board Members

Choose outside directors carefully. Not only do all internal directors have to feel good with the choice, but each director must have a clear plan of the contribution you expect. In ISSI's case, the connections both directors had, and the experience in business development, were the primary reasons they were brought aboard. Another common expectation is access to outside investors.

Fully understand why the prospective director wants to join the firm. For most experienced outside directors, money is not the main reason. More often it's a chance to help build a business. The pride of seeing "their" company succeed is real and powerful, and for some, provides some bragging rights at the country club.

Most importantly, a matching value set and a mature stable person are critical. Board-level disagreements over conduct and values are generally explosive. Diligently flush out everyone's values before bringing anyone on the board.

The Risks

Long-term control of your business is a big issue. The owners typically vote in directors once per year and thus do retain ultimate control. Still, having a bad director on board for a year can be a real problem, so choose carefully. ISSI today has 50% of the vote from outside directors, but Ceil and Dave said they aren't ready to go past that 50%. Together, they could still block the board from making a decision that they felt was ill-advised.

Although ISSI has never had such a problem, board members with secondary roles such as consultant have the possibility of conflict of interest—for example a board member pushing for a direction that increases the consulting work. But well-chosen board members with integrity, and a CEO who is watching the shop, mitigate this risk well.

It all boils down to how an entrepreneur gets high- level outside help. 1) You can hire that help (for big bucks, if you can find it); 2) you can give up ownership interests;

223

3) you can offer them a seat on the board; or 4) hire a consultant/mentor. Of course, combinations are common. Too many entrepreneurs easily give up pieces of their company. They later realize that it can be really hard and costly to recover that ownership. When looking for outside help, be sure to carefully consider the pros and cons of these four options.

Having an effective board with well-placed outside directors has taken some freedom from Ceil's ability to act independently. But she's gained freedoms that are far more valuable: the freedom from worrying if she personally has all the connections she needs to bring in business; the freedom from trying to make decisions in a vacuum; the freedom from worrying that she could ruin her business by making a big, bad decision on impulse; and the freedom of not having any more partners than when she started the business.

Key Takeaways

1. Having outside directors on your board is usually a good thing if done properly.
2. Directors should be selected strategically, and their special area of contribution should be acknowledged by all parties.
3. Treat your board as though you didn't control it, even if you do. The discipline of having to interact with an "independent" board is of great value in and of itself.

The Benefits of Peer Groups

(Continued from page 91)

Summary: Peer groups are an excellent way to learn lessons the easy way—from those who have already been through many of the trials of leadership. If the group has the right kind of peers and is well run, the cost-benefit is enormous.

Much as I wish it were otherwise, CEOs don't know it all. Worse yet, they are often faced with decisions where emotions, hidden agendas, and opinions are all mixed up with facts. Who do you talk to when you need to make a decision but the situation is not at all clear?

The answer is a group of peers—other CEOs like you who have been through the trials of business leadership. I'll share the benefits.

Holistic View. Other CEOs, like you, have to look at the organization as a whole. They by definition can't just look at the financial aspects, or the marketing aspects. Most of the big issues CEOs face have implications throughout the organization, and myopic views do not help bring closure.

Gut Feeling. We do so much to improve our brain and then we rely on our gut. Other CEOs, like you, have well-developed intuition. As you lay out the facts and circumstances as you see them, each of your peers will be feeling a gut reaction to your issue. Their minds will be synthesizing your facts with many earlier experiences that relate to what they are hearing from you. As they tell you their reactions, you can hear the commonality in their advice. If you're leaning toward a "yes" decision, and all ten of your peers warn you against "yes"—look out.

A group of peers you know and trust can also push you to pull the trigger on an action you know you should take but are dragging your feet. Sometimes we CEOs drag our feet out of fear, or uncertainty, or to avoid short-term pain. Or we're just stuck. The harassment, cajoling, or encouragement of your CEO group can be invaluable for getting you past that emotional barrier.

Fresh Perspectives. Another big advantage is that your peer group members have nothing to gain or lose by giving you their opinion. They should not be a customer, client, advisor, supplier, stockholder or board member. Their only currency is that if they give you honest advice, you'll return the favor when they need it. No hidden agendas. Likewise, you have nothing to lose in being completely honest with them and showing your soft, indecisive underbelly to them. They can't fire you (like your board can).

Occasionally, one of your peers in your CEO group will have specific expertise—like how to prepare for an IPO. That can add to the value, but it's not the main value. Most expert advice will come from consultants, or if you're a member of a larger CEO organization, you can reach into many other groups of CEOs to find those who have expert-level knowledge in a very specific area. At the very least, you may find referrals to great, proven consultants your peers have used.

Why don't all CEOs join a peer group? I've found that the main reasons are:

Arrogance. Some CEOs think that they know it all, and that most other peers don't have much more to contribute. This is nonsense. Just read some business journals and you'll find TONS of CEOs doing better than you and hundreds of amazing innovations they brought to the table. It's not just about fixing problems. It's about seeing things from a different perspective to uncover new opportunities. Some of the most valuable insights I've gotten from my peer group came from hearing the triumphs and issues of the *other* CEOs, then applying the lessons in my business.

Embarrassment. Some CEOs are afraid to show their underbelly. They are too embarrassed or insecure to say, "I don't know what to do," or "Here is what I am about to do, does anyone have any better ideas?" Joining such a group requires a commitment to be real—to be honest with your peers. If you put on the "I am fine and have no problems" show, it will be transparent and the group will likely reject you.

Too Busy. The number one most powerful asset that every CEO should tend to is their own knowledge and experience base. CEOs should have a training program of their own design. Many CEOs forget this and instead allow their own knowledge base to deplete with time (as everything does). Staying sharp and fresh, and making the best possible decisions should be your first investment of time and energy. It may not feel urgent, but it's really important.

Nobody Has My Problems. I know everyone feels they are special, and of course, you are. But your problems and challenges usually aren't that special. Somebody has been through it before, or at least something close enough to it to give you valuable advice and perspective. Even if you come up with some issues that your group doesn't help you with, getting great advice every other time, or every third time, is still a big benefit. Further, if you're part of a larger peer group with hundreds of members, you can reach beyond your own working group to find someone who can help you.

Not all peer groups are made equal. Some of the most important aspects to look for are:

A Great Facilitator. They keep the meetings on track and challenge the group to dig deeply and tackle key issues. They also serve to remind everyone to hold everyone else accountable over time.

New Blood When Needed. Members of peer groups come and go for various reasons. You need an organization that has new peers coming in and can put the right people in your group to keep things fresh. The right people are usually people with businesses of similar complexity to yours.

Members You (By and Large) Respect. In order to value the advice you get, you must respect the other members of your group. The right mix of people is difficult to find and maintain, so you need your peer organization actively managing this.

Regular Meetings. You can't bond with your peers if you don't meet with them regularly. Also, you will spend too much time "catching up" and not enough time tackling issues if you meet only every now and then. Nothing is more powerful than having 10 peer CEOs staring at you asking why you didn't do what you said you were going to do just 30 days ago. The thought of this can spur you into action.

Eagerness to Grow as CEOs. You and your peers in the group really should have a burning desire to do it better and the humility to know you have a lot to learn.

Strategy versus Tactics. For CEO-level peer groups, the focus has to be on strategy and vision to get the maximum benefit. Tactical issues can be handled outside the main meetings on a phone call/e-mail basis.

Personally, I've made back the membership dues and time investment from my membership in the Alliance of Chief Executives many-fold. Every year I think I am a smarter and better CEO, yet the more I meet other top CEOs, I learn still more. Thankfully, I love to learn.

How Deep in the Doghouse Do You Go?

(Continued from the endnote on page 117.)

Summary: Sometimes you must choose between coming clean as soon as possible and facing the consequences, or "hiding out" for a while and telling the truth later. This essay dives into this issue.

How deep into the doghouse do you want to go? Oftentimes, when faced with a problem, you can choose to take the hit up front and tackle it honestly, or you can cover it up, ignore it, dodge it, or hide from it in some way. For me the litmus test is whether avoidance will put you deeper into the doghouse, even if the trip to the doghouse is later than it might be.

Don't Make It Worse

The legal term is mitigating damage. That means that you do whatever you can as soon as you can to reduce the damage to all parties from growing further. For example, you realize that your outbound shipment just missed the ocean freighter. You know now that the machine you promised seven weeks from now will be late. If you tell the customer now, he can reduce his losses by taking other actions. You will mitigate his risks. On the other hand, if you don't tell him, what if he decommissions his old equipment in anticipation of a timely arrival? Then he discovers it's not on board when the ship arrives. Your late shipment hurt him, but your lack of honesty has cost him much more. Look out!

230

For me, the most important factor in deciding how much bad news to divulge when is the issue of mitigating damages. It's just wrong and bad business to not be candid and thus increase someone's pain and losses.
But what if there is no mitigating that can be done?

Your Partners

The next biggest factor for me is the nature of the relationship between the parties. The closer it is, the higher the obligation for complete openness and honesty. Anyone you regard as a business partner (and that could be a legal partner, or a trusted vendor, key employee, spouse, etc.) should be entitled to know the straight skinny. Keeping things secret from them when you know they'll care is detrimental to the relationship in the long term.

Now maybe when you get bad news just before a weekend, you could wait until Monday to share it. Or if they just had a death in the family, you give it a week to let them become ready for the next blow. Being kind is certainly acceptable. But holding out because you're afraid of their reaction, or because it may cost you is not good practice.

Time Is Pressing

Sometimes the passage of time makes the decision for us. If a decision needs to be made with another, it's paramount that you share the situation with them soon enough to allow them to fully participate in the decision.

231

Getting Credit for Recovery

One of the best ways to build client and customer relationships is to recover from a blunder in a fantastic fashion, exceeding expectations. I can't tell you how many times this has been the key factor in solidifying a relationship for me or my company. Not that I ever purposefully messed up to have this opportunity, but that when it happened, I dove right into the fire and kept at it until all was fixed. This usually costs money, but it's better than advertising!

If you and your company follow a policy of forthrightness, a reputation will develop along those lines. Over time (a few years), you'll find that people trust you more and more quickly. It's a big advantage.

Gentleness

Sometimes that bad news isn't about what you did wrong, but about what they did wrong. Problem employees pop to mind. While being blunt, direct and self-critical are great techniques when you're admitting to your own company's failings, being gentle, tactful and caring are the way to go when it's they who blew it. Just be sure they get the message, so that the problem doesn't continue.

All at Once?

Sometimes you can't rip away too many old beliefs and expectations too soon. You have to do it one piece at a time, giving the other party time to absorb and acknowledge the issues one at a time. Sometimes that means not admitting quite all that you know right away. Just make sure you're not doing it to save yourself a headache, or that the delay isn't causing increasing damages for anyone.

When Is Telling a Lie OK?

In my book, it's rare if ever that it's the right thing to do to lie. This article is really about what to do when you're already headed toward the "doghouse" and is in the context of business—what we do to make money. So lying to save a life (which is certainly understandable) isn't part of what we're talking about.

Lying when it's easy to detect and you'll likely get caught is clearly a bad idea and is the fastest way to destroy your credibility. The other nasty problem with lying is that you often have to keep lying to maintain the story, which means you're being bad over and over again. Pretty soon you can be faced with just a few options, none of which is easy.

Even when lying is of little consequence to you down the road, patterns of dishonesty develop into a bad reputation and over time, you'll pay for it.

The Chess Game

Whenever I'm faced with situations that look like they require uncomfortable disclosures, I look at it like a chess game. If I take one action, what will they do, then what would I do, and how does that path play out. Then, I repeat the process with all of my alternatives. It certainly helps clarify what to do.

All about Earn-Outs

(Continued from page 118)

Summary: A common element in buying and selling businesses is where the seller gets paid more if certain goals are achieved by the buyer in the years following the sale. This is called an "earn-out" and can be tricky and uncertain. But they do hold the opportunity of earning more from a sale over time.

Nobody knows what the future holds. Nobody. What has happened in the past can help to understand what the future may hold, but it is no guarantee. Throw in to the mix a change of ownership of a business, and there is even more reason to worry that the future will be different from the past.

This issue is at the crux of valuing any business being sold. The buyers of the world are investing money in hopes of getting a good return in the uncertain future. What happened in the past won't do them any good.

The sellers of the world have worked hard and have created a track record documenting the viability of the business over time. They want to get a fair return for all that hard work and investment over the years.

Both positions are correct and fair. But the price of the business, as figured by buyer and seller, usually comes out with a gap. Part of the gap can be offset by unequal eagerness on the part of the seller and buyer. In other words, a buyer who really wants to buy will get more generous, or a seller eager to sell backs off a bit.

When they are still apart, an earn-out is often a solution. In short, an earn-out is a payment made only if a certain condition is met. For example, if sales in year 2 really do hit 22 million, then the seller will be paid an additional 2 million.

Yes, the sellers should feel uncomfortable with earn-outs. And the buyers will be happy to offer them. Sometimes if you want the deal consummated, you have to accept some portion of the price being an earn-out.

Here are some really important considerations.

1. What portion should be an earn-out? Certainly if the seller is claiming big hockey-stick growth in the future, he can't expect to be paid guaranteed dollars for that. An earn-out seems fair. But earn-outs are very risky and are often not paid for a variety of reasons. Only a high-risk future should be offset with earn-outs.

2. Earn-outs are based on conditions, and those conditions must be defined very clearly. This is a huge, very troublesome matter. Defining them by net sales sounds easy, but what if the new owners cut the product development budget by 50%? They'll have the right to do it and not pay the earn-out—unless you've put in the contract an agreed amount to spend on product development. Earn-outs based on EBITDA or net profit are horribly contentious calculations. What if you, the

seller and agreed-upon CEO of the business after the sale, are fired? Do the earn-outs then pay immediately? The variables go on and on. Think them through carefully and with an experienced deal maker, lest everyone enrich lawyers after the fact.

3. As a seller, if you never get your earn-out, how will you feel?

4. As a seller, have you bargained your hardest to minimize the earn-out? Fixed guaranteed payments over time are much more secure than an earn-out (but still not nearly as secure as cash on the barrelhead). Can you shift some earn-out to fixed payments?

5. Have you carefully researched the buyer's historical performance on earn-outs promised to past sellers?

If the business you are selling is strong, with excellent past performance (from an independent point of view), then you should insist on a large guaranteed amount for the business, with a little upside above the base as an earn-out. On the other hand, if your performance has been mixed and the buyer has offered a fixed amount that is too low for you, then look at an earn-out as a possibility to make up some of the difference.

Be assured that earn-outs often cause ill will between the seller and the buyer over time. There are just so many things that can go wrong or can be viewed from different perspectives. If having a good relationship with the other party is important post-sale, work really hard to avoid or minimize earn-outs.

Of course, relative power trumps all. If you've just GOT to sell, you won't have much ability to affect the outcome. Just the same, if you've GOT to buy, you'll surely end up overpaying.

Key Takeaways

1. From the seller's point of view, earn-outs are not very good and are a risky way to be paid for your business. From a buyer's point of view, it's a good tool to bridge the gap between the value of what the seller says will happen and what actually happens.
2. Be sure to clarify the rules around the earn-out, keeping in mind that the buyer would rather not pay the earn-out, and the seller really wants the earn-out.
3. If maintaining a good relationship between seller and buyer after the deal is done is important, try and minimize or eliminate the earn-out.

Use of Advisors in Acquisitions

(From comment on page 123)

Summary: Most CEOs will need and want advisors to help them in their M&A efforts, but how you work with those advisors is a critical issue and depends in large part on your skill set.

No matter how smart you are, your biggest enemy is what you don't know. Unless you've spent a lot of time doing M&A work, I guarantee you there is a lot you don't know about this process.

I'm not just talking about legal jargon. I'm talking about how the parties "sniff" each other out, how the negotiations take place, what you should expect to give and get. It doesn't stop there. There are many subtleties. The worst thing you can do is take a hard position on an issue that is completely outside the normal way deals get done. It shows you to be an amateur, and it could either unravel the deal or cost you money.

This is why *great* advisors are invaluable. They guide you through times when you have no experience yourself. How you work with your advisor depends on a number of factors. In general, I believe that the buyer or seller should themselves do as much as possible in the areas they can do well. A buyer or seller could be one person in a small or mid-size firm, or a team of people employed by a larger firm.

How Well Do You Show?

Since you are kind enough to be reading my book, I'll assume you're a great person. But does that come through when meeting with the other party? Do you come across as friendly, very knowledgeable, reasonable, and overall someone they really would want to do a transaction with? If so, you should be center stage. If you show poorly, then you'll need an advisor who can be more of the interface. But I'll warn you now, it's probably not your lawyer.

Do You Know When You Need Help?

If you're the "front" person, you'll be out there working the deal. In any given meeting, issues will come up that you didn't anticipate. You'll have to make split-second decisions about whether to tackle the issue, or say, "Let me think about that and we'll take it back up at the next meeting," which is code for, "I don't know what to do and I need to ask my advisor what he/she thinks first." If you're good at seeing the potential potholes quickly and sidestepping, then you can leave your advisor home most of the time.

How Well Do You Listen and Take Advice?

The best kind of advice you can get is advice that helps you learn the M&A process and how to make decisions. Rather than having an advisor just tell you that seven million is a fair price, you'll want to learn how a "fair price" is generally calculated. So when you're at the table on your own, to hammer out the price, and a key variable changes (say EBITDA adjustments get changed), you'll be able to amend your offer on the spot—not have to go back to the advisor for a recalculation. If working this way—doing lots of learning—is good for you, again, you can leave your advisor in the background.

Can You Be the Analyst?

Big important aspects of M&A have to do with interfacing with the other side. But a lot of analysis work has to be done as well. If you are buying a business in your own industry and you know your business, you should be deeply involved in this aspect. Where many can use help is in the normal measures of value for any business. Applying those measures properly is essential to valuation. But when it comes to forecasting the future of the business, the fundamentals of that forecast are usually deep within the specifics of that very business. Things like future market acceptance of the product or service, industry trends and competition make a world of difference. Most M&A advisors don't bring industry-specific knowledge. A good M&A advisor does know how to learn fairly quickly and has good horse sense for when he does or doesn't understand a business.

Are You a Lawyer?

Probably not. To do an M&A deal you do need a lawyer to keep you protected from current and future pitfalls. Understand that every deal can be divided into two sections—business issues and legal issues. Business issues are how much you pay (or receive), how much risk you are willing to accept, whether you should insist on more or less security for what you will be owed, and so on. Legal issues are the wording of the deal documents, making sure your deal cannot be unraveled down the road due to technicalities, complying with the law, and avoiding any "surprise" problems coming down the road via the legal system.

A lawyer's job is not to help you with business issues. I do realize that some lawyers have done so many deals that they have expertise in these matters too, and if that truly is the case and they can act in both roles, that's fine. But too often, the lawyer who tries to act in both roles really worries too early about avoiding ALL risk, "fights" for you on the legal details way too early, and drives the parties apart. What is supposed to happen is that the parties come together on interpersonal and business terms, get a rough outline of the deal, then let the lawyers "pick over" the details. Some of those details are REALLY important and do get fought over, but when the parties feel like they're almost there—the deal more often withstands controversy.

Are You a CPA?

A third type of advisor is an accountant. Once the business points are generally agreed upon, and the lawyer is hammering out the legalese, the CPAs get involved. Their focus is generally assessing the tax effect on their client, then suggesting ways to structure the deal to minimize taxes. This is complicated, and understanding the many taxation rules at both state and federal levels is critical. Deal structure can vary widely and can have a HUGE impact on the real cost of a deal for both sides.

It's Your Deal

Never forget that it's your deal, not your advisor's deal. I do strongly advocate having great advisors to help you in your M&A activities. I also strongly advise listening to them carefully and peppering them with questions until you fully understand their position. BUT NEVER ABDICATE CONTROL. You make the final decision, you decide what steps should be taken to have the outcome you desire. It's your deal.

Key Takeaways

1. You must know what you don't know—to avoid stepping into problems blindly.
2. You or your internal team should do as much as your skills and competencies allow, and work hard on learning from the advisors you hire so you can build your skill set.
3. Never abdicate control—it's your deal and you must call the shots after listening to your advisors.

Dealing with Banks
(Continued from page 127.)

Summary:
Banks look to lend money to companies with good to great financials. If you're on the good end of the spectrum, this essay will help you understand how to work with a bank so that they understand you and your businesses complexities.

Most CEOs have a love-hate relationship with the notion of borrowing from the bank. Sometimes bankers are eager to loan and friendly. At other times, they are demanding, even aggressive in collecting money. The truth is they are businesses themselves, looking for ways to make profit through money lending. Get used to it.

Banks partner with businesses as suppliers of cash only when they are convinced that it is a smart and profitable deal for them. When being your cash partner looks too risky, they run for the hills—and they should!

Every bank loves making loans to "golden" companies, but no commercial bank wants the high-risk loans. But much of the profit for a bank comes from the loans made in grey-area situations, where it takes an understanding of the business beyond the financial statements to make a good decision. So it's the companies that are in the middle range, or "gray area," where it's critical to convince the bank that your business has very low risk.

Will They Hear You?

All banks make a good show of listening to you. But only some banks really hear what you have to say. Your goal is to work with someone senior enough at the bank that their opinion matters. Someone experienced enough to understand your business and able to write their perceptions down in a credible form. You see, every loan a bank makes has a narrative in the file written by the bank, explaining why the loan is prudent. *This gives life to the numbers.* The bank's auditors and the regulatory agencies will read that narrative. Making sure your story is told well in that narrative is critical.

The bank cares deeply about your ability to run your business well. It's key to paying back the loan. What can you do to prove your business competency? Right from the start, show them that you are financially savvy; understand your own business as well as the nature of the banking relationship. Be forthright about your situation— especially anything that they could discover on their own through analyzing the statements. Trying to hide something that they will discover on their own is a fast way to damage their trust in you or their faith in your competency.

Most bankers want to know everything about your business. Most bankers will say, "It always works best when we have regular dialogue with our customers." Yet most CEOs worry about unnecessarily spooking the bank. My advice is to share small issues and victories with them on a quarterly or bi-annual basis. If anything major happens, you probably need to share this with them as well. Keeping them updated shows that you are in control of your business, not vice-versa.

Bankability

Knowing how bankable you are is always critical. And it's not a yes or no. Some businesses are incredibly creditworthy—anyone would loan them money. Others are fairly bankable, and some are barely bankable. After the bank renews your line of credit each year, be sure to ask them their opinion of your firm's creditworthiness versus where you stood a year ago. The idea is not to wait until the bank calls your loan to deal with eroding financials. You should solicit feedback from your bank so you can take action well before it's too late.

When a bank has concerns, the first thing they do is to ask for more frequent reporting. It helps them catch issues before they are too late and gives them time to act as a consultant to the borrower, often restructuring debt or making other suggestions. If your bank is concerned enough to ask for more frequent reporting, pay attention and figure out what you need to improve.

Ratings

Banks rate every loan. Being rated "pass" means your loan is OK. But when you slip, the first downward rating is "pass-watch," then "sub-standard," then "non-performing," then "loss." If you're an existing borrower, they might renew you on a watch status, but if you're substandard or below, they have already pulled your loan.

Keeping up a second banking relationship is a great idea. You may have only a few accounts there, or a minor credit facility. But any history with a bank is important. If your primary lender has issues with your loan, you'll have a second bank that already knows you—a big help if you need to switch lenders.

Realize that if your financial position is so poor that banks are afraid to loan you money, then no amount of talk, positioning, or anything else will help you get the loan. So if borrowing money is what you know you need to do, run your business such that your financials will look solid from a bank's perspective.

Key Takeaways

1. Choose a bank where you have direct contact with someone whose opinion matters at the decision point.
2. Keep up communications with the bank—appearing less than forthright is never good for the relationship.
3. Monitor over time how healthy your bank thinks you are. If they think your bank-ability is slipping, start planning other options.

The Roving CEO

(Continued from page 135.)

(Continued from page 135.)

Summary: **The CEO must keep an eye on each department in his/her company to sense which one is struggling, then dive into that department to pull it forward.**

Business requires that you do a lot of things right. Just like an eight-cylinder engine, when all eight cylinders are firing perfectly, you've got the most power. In my mind, the different business functions of a company are just like the cylinders in an engine.

It takes constant tending to keep them all working perfectly in harmony, and the CEO must be the chief mechanic. They get out of whack when the business changes and systems and/or managers are outgrown. They get out of whack when new products or services are added, stressing some departments more than others. They get out of whack from wear and the passage of time.

On a regular basis, you must assess the performance of each department and take action to assist the department that is lagging the most and is threatening to hold the company back from its objectives. You'll be acting like a consultant (but with real organizational power), fixing the problems that exist and bringing the department forward so that it is one of the better-performing departments. Once accomplished, you can neglect it a bit while you change the focus of your attention to the next lagging department.

Depending on the size of the business, and the strength of the department's leadership, you will get your hands more or less dirty. More than likely, you'll get involved with hiring and firing of people, processes, reviewing assumptions, assessing hard-to-assess factors (like the marketplace), and making some decisions that your managers are too afraid to make. Since you're the CEO, you naturally do all this in the context of the bigger picture.

Don't misunderstand: You're always playing coach, guiding the people you have in charge of each department. It may be that if you have a star leader of a department, they rarely become your lagging department. Wonderful! That's the kind of department leader you want to have in all your departments. In fact, if the same department keeps lagging, then you probably do need to look at changing that department's leader. But with growing companies in particular, the problems and challenges are not evenly distributed in all departments. Put your energy in where it counts.

But don't get sucked in. The CEO should not get too tied down with day-to-day operations. (This is all relative to size, of course) Coming in to help a department doesn't mean that you end up doing their job for them for any length of time. It means you go in, innovate and assist, pass the knowledge on, then get free of it so that you are free to move on.

Having said all this, don't make it worse by making your own wrong decisions. Most CEOs are not great at all things. If you see that a department needs help but your skill set isn't up to it, then find someone you trust who does have that skill set and work together with them to dive in. You still make the key judgments and are deeply involved, but with a person at your side advising and assisting you.

Key Takeaways:

1. Know that as time passes and your business grows, challenges will hit departments unevenly, and the laggards will need help.
2. It's your job to act as an internal consultant, diving in when needed to effect lasting change and improvement.
3. As soon as possible, you must pull back out of the details of that department so that you are ready to help the next lagging department or tackle other challenges.

Staying Sane when Things Go Wrong

(*From page 137.*)

Summary: Keeping a productive mindset when times are tough is critical to being able to fight your way out. I share my techniques and approach.

Let me go on record as saying that I am against hard times. That I believe that we should pass a law that forbids things going wrong. Smoking cigarettes and eating trans-fats are bad for your health, and so are hard times. Let's start a petition...*All right, enough of the whining.*

Tough times are part of life, and we CEOs and leaders get the big bucks in part because we lead our followers through tough times and back out again. Plus, without challenges, we'd never get the gratification of triumph.

What happens in a leader's head during tough times? How did the military leader ride his horse at the front of the charge, knowing the risks he and his men faced?

The biggest and most fundamental truth is that *the leader must know himself or herself.*

You must consciously examine what activities or thoughts have helped you in the past get by things like despair, immobilizing fear, unproductive angry thinking, panic or other harmful mindsets or actions.

After honest and regular introspection, you're ready for the next step. *You must lead yourself.* It's the same as leading others. You decide what needs to happen, and you ask, challenge and direct yourself to do it. For me, the deeper, more strategic version of self-leadership happens at quiet times, such as before bed or in the shower. But the tactical applications of leading oneself happen throughout the day—just as in the story when I pasted a smile on before charging into my meeting with a customer.

Sounds like mind control? It is. But hey, it's your own mind.

I do think that the CEO has to see reality, no matter how ugly it is. He or she has to grapple with it and struggle to find a way to make the outcome better. But once a good path through it has been found, the focus must change.

The new focus is moving the company along the path you've defined. On day one (after being confronted with a problem), it may be true that the situation is horrible. But most can't function well while dwelling on "horrible," and that includes me. Instead, I dwell on what I must do today to move down the path. By the end of the day, if I've moved forward on my path, I've had a good day and I take pleasure in that. True, if I stopped and looked at the big picture again, I might see that it's only a tiny bit better than horrible, which is still horrible. But doing that hurts me—it takes away the sense of opportunity I gave myself when I focused on seeing how far down the path to survival I could get each day.

Yes, I am suggesting that you stick your head in the sand for short periods of time. It keeps you from panic and other non-productive emotions. A short period of time might be a few hours or a day or a week. Never keep it in the sand for too long, lest you fail to change course when it's essential.

Now the "path to survival" doesn't always mean the path to unfathomable riches. Depending on how horrible the situation is, it might be the path to keeping your house and car while the business is liquidated in bankruptcy. That would be a step up from losing your house, car, and business. I am absolutely a realist, and I do fully believe that when the chips are down, you must fundamentally make a go or no-go decision, then carry it out. Being "Pollyanna" about a crash-and-burn situation will only make the wreckage worse.

The truth is, in tough times it often looks worse than it is, and a business can survive amazingly bad situations if the leader and his or her team keep working to fix it. If you really have assessed the situation and can see the light at the end of the tunnel, then go for it, and have faith in yourself and your team. And it really is faith. Without that faith, you'll lose many battles you could have won.

Personally, I have very good stamina in a struggle. I can work very hard for very long periods of time without wearing down. Often, a vacation feels like I'm not working, not making progress on my path to success. But I've learned over the years that time away from the battle on occasion does move me down the path, because I always return to the fray from a different mental and emotional place, on a different trajectory. It's as though my mind had the time to float up to the 10,000-foot view and the space to re-analyze the situation. Be sure to use getting away as a tool to help you in tough times.

I am a big advocate of focusing your energies, especially in tough times. But sometimes the way out isn't the apparent path—it's a surprise "win" that offsets the problem. So be open to serendipity (making desirable discoveries by accident). Allocate a small portion of your time to chasing down opportunities that might be long shots or good in the long term. Chances are significant that you will survive your current crisis and will be needing and wanting rich opportunities when the future arrives. So keep planting the seeds that will grow into your future. And tending those seeds—gardening just a little each week—can be a welcome respite from the daily grind of tough times.

Afterword

This book is billed as an acquisitions book. And while there are some special issues in acquisitions, the truth is that the skills, behaviors and beliefs for being successful in business are truly the subject of this book.

An acquisition is a nice case study that forces all the contexts of business into one compressed example. For instance, if you look at the time I put into getting to know Phil Ginsburg so I could buy his business—why shouldn't you put that same time into getting to know your business partner or your top executives? Likewise, if you look at the rigor with which I dug into the financial transactions of the company, wouldn't you want to do the same to your own business periodically?

The challenge then, in both acquisitions and business in general, is to become competent at the blend of soft skills and hard skills, while being able to assess the match between opportunities and your vision of success.

That's quite a challenge, and that's exactly what keeps me interested in the field of business. But most importantly, where are *your* greatest challenges as a business leader, and what is *your* plan to overcome them?

About the Author

Robert Sher is the principal of CEO to CEO, an advisory practice dedicated to the world in which CEOs work. His CEO case study columns are published in the *East Bay Business Times* and the *San Jose Business Journal* as well as on the Alliance of Chief Executives Advisory e-Board. He is a speaker for audiences of entrepreneurs, executives, business owners and C-level executives.

Robert Sher serves as a Director of the Alliance of Chief Executives. In 2007 he focused on building systems, processes and activities that facilitate increased member communication and mutual support, in particular among members in different working groups.

Robert was CEO/President and a founder of Bentley Publishing Group. He was at the helm from 1984 through 2006, and this industry-leading decorative poster publishing firm has grown significantly, including four acquisitions since 1999.

He writes a regular column for leading magazines in the wall décor industry and the hobby industry and is a founder and Chairman of the Art Copyright Coalition, a worldwide organization fighting to stop copyright infringement of visual artists. He also holds a leadership role in an education industry startup, S is for Science.

Between 1995 and 2000, he was a Lecturer under contract with St. Mary's College, teaching Entrepreneurship and

Small Business Management to hundreds of graduate students in the MBA and Executive MBA programs.

Robert Sher received a B.S. in Business from Hayward State University and an MBA from St. Mary's College, where he received the Jack Saloma award. He is married to Renee and father of two children, Jessica and Ben, and lives in the San Francisco Bay Area.